Contents

Chapter 1: Why Knit?

3
The Top Reasons to Start Knitting Now

Chapter 2: Getting Started

7
Materials, Tips, Organization

10
Slip Knot

11
Knit Stitch (English)

12
Knit Stitch (Continental)

13
Purl Stitch (English)

14
Purl Stitch (Continental)

15
Binding Off & Finishing

Chapter 3: Next Steps

17
Increases & Decreases

18
Ribbing

19
Gauge

20
Abbreviations & Schematics

22
Fixing Mistakes

Chapter 4: A Fine Finish

26
Blocking

27
Seaming

30
Picking Up Stitches

31
Buttonholes

Chapter 5: A Basic Stitch Sampler

35
Ribbing

37
Basic Textures

40
Lace Knitting

42
Cables & Colorwork

Chapter 6: Fu.

46 Yin Scarf 46 Yin & Yang Scarf 47 His Hats

47 Her Hats 48 Trellis Shawl 49 Mohair Poncho

50 Baby Blanket 51 Chevron Afghan 52 Easy Pullover

54 Boatneck Pullover 56 Shawl Collar Cardigan 58 Baby Sweater

60 Shawl Collar Pullover 62 Garter-Ridge Socks 64 Baby Booties

For pattern inquiries, please visit: www.go-crafty.com
Instructional photographs feature *Lion* by Lion Brand Yarn in #123 Seaspray, #140 Rose, and #158 Banana (except pages 58–59).
All photography Dan Howell (with exception to page 59, Paul Amato).

Chapter One
why knit?

Welcome to the world of knitting!

By picking up a pair of knitting needles and a ball of yarn, you're embarking on an exciting journey, one that has the potential to bring you joy for many years to come. Knitting brings out your creative side, offers a sense of accomplishment and even soothes your nerves at the end of a long day. It's portable, versatile, and full of endless possibilities.

The Top Reasons to Start Knitting Now

1. Knitting Relieves Stress

According to Dr. Mona Lisa Schultz, author of *The New Feminine Brain* (Free Press, 2005), knitting has a relaxing effect on the brain similar to the anti-anxiety drug Valium. WARNING: Knitting may be addictive!

2. Knitting Is the New Yoga

Knitting has been dubbed the new yoga. But don't cancel your membership at the studio just yet—the two go hand in hand. The Kripalu Center for Yoga & Health in Lenox, Massachusetts, offers classes combining knitting and yoga taught by longtime knitter and yoga practitioner Karen Allen, who feels that the two practices perfectly complement one another. Medical studies prove her right. "Like meditation or prayer, knitting allows for the passive release of stray thoughts," says Dr. Herbert Benson of Harvard Medical School and author of *The Relaxation Response* (William Morrow, 1975). "The rhythmic and repetitive quality of the stitching, along with the sound of needles clicking, resembles a calming mantra," Dr. Benson explains. "The mind can wander while still focusing on one task." So if your shoulders get tight from too much knitting, try a downward-facing dog.

3. Knitting Provides Mental and Creative Stimulation

Feeling a little fuzzy? Grab some yarn, fuzzy or not, and a pair of needles to clear the cobwebs away. Recent research suggests that a brain workout (like the one provided by counting rows) on a regular basis can greatly reduce the risk of developing dementia. Working with rainbow colors and sensual textures also gets the creative juices flowing. Just walking into a great yarn shop can create sensory overload! There's no need to be overwhelmed, though—luckily, yarn shop owners are some of the most helpful folks on the planet!

4. Knitting Is Good for Your Health

The therapeutic benefits of knitting have long been put into use. During World War I, hospitalized soldiers learned to knit as a way to keep their minds off painful injuries. Knitting involves just the right combination of simple repetitive hand motions and mental focus to make it useful in a variety of rehabilitation situations, from strokes to head injuries, according to Robin Hedeman of the Kessler Institute of Rehabilitation in New Jersey. It's used as an aid to smoking cessation and even weight loss. "It might seem ironic since knitting is a sedentary activity, but working on a knitting project can help take the focus off food," states addictions counselor Karen Mell. Balance the sedentary side of knitting with frequent stretch breaks and walks to the yarn store.

Don't let arthritis keep you from picking up the needles! You may find that the repetitive hand movements involved in knitting keep your joints lubricated. Try using wooden or bamboo needles and take frequent stretching breaks. Please check with your doctor before starting if your condition is severe.

5. Knitting Is Portable, Productive, and Oh, So Glamorous

OK, you're probably getting tired of hearing about which actress has been spotted knitting this week. Julia Roberts, Cameron Diaz, and Hilary Swank all knit. The image of movie stars stitching on the sets of Hollywood productions may seem a long way from the ancient shepherds who knit while watching their flocks or sailors whiling away the endless hours aboard ships knitting caps, but you get the concept. Knitting is a great way to occupy your down time. It's the perfect antidote for those of us who feel a certain touch of guilt watching TV or waiting for a plane or train. Knitting also seems to shorten those endless waits in doctors' offices.

Note for frequent flyers: The government's Transportation Security Administration includes knitting needles and crochet hooks on its official list of approved items for both carry-on and checked luggage for domestic travel. If you're traveling abroad, check with your airline to see if there are restrictions in the country you're visiting. If they don't allow knitting needles as carry-on, stash your project in your checked luggage. On-plane knitting etiquette tip: use shorter wooden or bamboo needles—and no elbowing your seatmate!

6. Knitting Is Ageless, Timeless, and Unisex

Marge Westcott, a 51-year-old Brooklyn, New York, resident, recently asked her niece to teach her how to knit. Sarah Westcott, 30, a location scout and avid knitter, learned knitting from her grandmother on the other side of the family, who in turn had learned from her mother. "I know it seems like the traditional roles are reversed, but I never took the time to learn when I was younger," Marge explains. "I kept noticing all the terrific projects Sarah was knitting and finally I just couldn't wait!" Now they spend Saturday afternoons visiting the many wonderful yarn shops New York City has to offer. Judith L. Swartz, author of *Hip to Knit* (Interweave Press, 2002), has also observed this trend: "Lately I've noticed more girls teaching their grandmothers to knit, or at least giving them a refresher course, than the other way around!" Whoever teaches you (and we hope it's this book!), chances are you'll soon have an opportunity to pass it on.

Historians disagree about the exact beginnings of the craft of knitting, but whether it began in ancient Egypt or medieval Europe, one thing is clear—knitting is here to stay. Although many think of knitting as women's work, throughout history men have often been the star knitters. So, gentlemen, why not join shepherds, sailors, and soldiers of the past and jump on the knitting bandwagon? Be a part of today's resurgence of knitting among both sexes and keep tradition alive.

7. Knitting Provides an Opportunity to Give Back to the Community

A quick web search found almost one hundred organizations that distribute hand-knitted items to folks in need. Afghans for Afghans sends handmade blankets to displaced Afghani families; Warm Up America creates cozy afghans one square at a time. Check out resources in your local community. Places of worship, hospitals, and civic clubs often have programs organized to distribute layette items to premature babies, warm clothing to homeless families, and knitted toys to children in need.

8. Knitting Improves Your Wardrobe and Provides Countless Gift-Giving Ideas

Have an urge to augment your wardrobe with fabulous knitwear or expecting a new baby in the family? Whatever the inspiration to pick up the needles, most new knitters start with a frenzy of scarf making and graduate to more advanced projects such as hats, afghans, and sweaters. Yarn shop owners all over agree that one of the biggest motivations to learn knitting is the longing to make gifts. And let's not forget, knits are forgiving—they stretch—so they're flattering to all figures!

9. Knitting Can Be Good for Your Social Life

Your newfound hobby can help you meet new friends of all ages and discover a sense of community. Check out the library, community colleges, and yarn shops for classes and knitting clubs. Or consider joining a knitting guild through the Knitting Guild Association and be connected to a nationwide network of knitting groups. The group's website, www.tkga.com, provides a search by zip code to help you find a guild near you. You'll have instant access to its newsletter, educational programs, and conventions.

10. Knitting Promotes Shopping and Travel Opportunities

It's not just the fabulous yarn shops you'll be visiting on a regular basis. Think of the tote bags you'll want for all your knitting projects and the baskets to store the yarn. You might even decide to purchase a stylish new easy chair for your knitting comfort.

Finally, in case you still need convincing, consider that most places you visit virtually anywhere in the world have a textile tradition. You'll have a new reason to broaden your horizons—knitting research! Remember, yarn is highly packable—so be sure to purchase souvenir skeins wherever you go!

Chapter Two
getting started

Now that you know the benefits of learning to knit, it's time to join the knitting boom!

Before you get started, you'll want to do a little market research. Visit your local YARN SHOP or the yarn section of a craft store to get a feel for what's out there, then start gathering supplies. Spend some time searching the Internet checking for knitting-oriented WEBSITES. These days you can truly shop for just about anything without leaving your desk, but most knitters can't resist the visual, tactile, and SOCIAL PLEASURES of their local yarn shop. Introduce yourself as a new knitter. You'll be thrilled at the enthusiastic response, and this connection will come in handy later if you run trouble and need some TECHNICAL HELP.

Living in the Material World

One of the most compelling reasons for jumping on the knitting bandwagon is the amazing abundance of fabulous knitting materials available from knitting shops, craft chains, and online suppliers.

It's a Big Yarn-iverse Out There!

If you're like most knitting novices, you are chomping at the bit to run out and purchase bags full of novelty yarns (the ones with all the texture), bulky yarns (yes, the big fat ones), and luxury fibers (like cashmere, angora, and alpaca). Be patient. We recommend learning with a basic yarn—it's easier to work with, doesn't split, and is more forgiving. And choose a light color—it's easier to see.

You'll soon learn that yarn is organized by weight (thickness) and ranges from super-fine to super-bulky. For your first project, we recommend a worsted or mid-weight yarn. Nearly all yarn comes with a ball band or label clearly stating the recommended needle size and gauge (more on that later). Always save the ball band, as it is the source of lots of useful information, including fiber content and care instructions. Speaking of balls, most commercial yarn you'll run across will be in the form of a ball (round) or skein (oblong) with the yarn pulling out from the center. Occassionally you'll find a yarn you love that's "put up" in hank form, which will have to be wound into a ball. If the yarn shop can't do it for you, enlist a friend (or kid) to act as a human "niddy noddy" (hank holder) while you wind the ball.

You'll Need Needles

Knitting needles come in a wide variety of materials. Traditional metal needles make that classic knitting "click" that remind many of us of Grandma, but they can be cold to the touch. Plastic needles are lightweight and widely available. Today the favorites of most knitters seem to be wood and bamboo needles, which have a warm earthy feel to them, and the rounded ends don't split the yarn. Bamboo is flexible and the needles warm as you work with them. Wooden needles, available in everything from birch to ebony, are elegant to the eye and pleasing to the touch, but tend to be pricey. It's a good idea to experiment and see which materials feel most comfortable to you.

Shed a Little Light on the Subject

Natural light is the most relaxing for the eyes and allows you to work for longer periods of time. But let's face it, you're not always going to be sitting in the sunroom to knit. Luckily, there are attractive lamps on the market that won't make your living room like an operating room. To avoid eyestrain, take frequent breaks, close your eyes from time to time, and try "palming" (gently rest palms on closed eyes for a few moments). Oh, and drink plenty of water—it helps keep the eyes lubricated.

Oh, My Aching Hands

Worried that knitting will trigger repetitive stress conditions, such as carpal tunnel syndrome, or aggravate arthritis? Don't be; According to Shannon Whetstone Mescher, spokesperson for the Arthritis Foundation, knitting doesn't cause arthritis, nor does it make it worse. She suggests you check with your physician if your condition is severe but says, "The benefits of movement, especially keeping joints lubricated, usually outweigh the downside." She recommends frequent breaks, hand stretches, and massage. For the most part, the same applies to carpal tunnel sufferers. Those with constant hand pain from either condition might want to try specially designed fingerless support gloves. Available at craft stores, these support and warm the hands to minimize fatigue, pain, and swelling.

If your hands tend to be dry (whose aren't?), be sure to use a rich, emollient hand cream to keep your skin from cracking and catching on yarn. Keep a nail file handy for smoothing rough nails and preventing snags in your yarn. Fun fact: Although sheep's wool contains lanolin, an ingredient in many hand creams (knitters of yesteryear had the softest hands), most of today's yarns have been cleaned so thoroughly that they contain only a trace amount of this natural skin softener.

Organizing Principles

Once you have a few knitting projects underway, you'll need a system for curbing yarn chaos. One way to add method to your newfound madness is to initiate the "tote bag system"—a separate bag for each project you've begun, containing yarn, needles, and the pattern you are using. Keep your pattern in a plastic sleeve protector and when you're done with the project, insert the pattern into a loose-leaf binder or knitting notebook along with other vital info pertaining to that project—ball bands, a note of where you bought the yarn, and a snapshot of the finished project and the recipient. You'll be able to look back and easily see what you made and for whom. Many yarn shops sell knitter's journals made especially for this purpose. Organize needles by size in a case designed for the job. That way, each time you need size 10 needles, you won't be tempted to run out to buy another pair because you can't remember where you put them.

More Tools of the Trade

When you're first learning to knit, there's not much you need other than knitting needles and a few balls of yarn. Once you move onto more advanced projects, you may find some of these inexpensive gadgets infinitely helpful:

1 Small, sharp scissors for snipping off loose ends.

2 Large-eyed, blunt-tipped yarn or tapestry needles for seaming and weaving in yarn ends.

3 An assortment of pins—rust-proof T-pins for blocking, straight pins for seaming, and safety pins for marking rows.

4 Flexible, non-stretch tape measure, for accurate measurements.

5 A variety of crochet hooks, handy for picking up dropped stitches as well as adding decorative trim.

6 A plastic or metal stitch gauge—more on that when we discuss gauge in Chapter 3.

7 Double-pointed cable needles to hold stitches while you work a cable pattern.

(You'll need a few other items for blocking your first project, but we'll get to that in Chapter 4.)

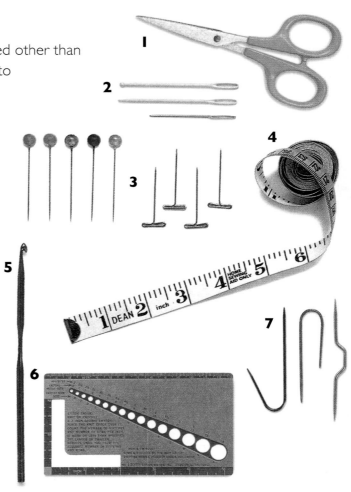

Please Be Seated

Before you begin knitting, pay attention to where you'll be sitting. There's no need to get out and buy a high-end ergonomic chair, but if you're going to be knitting for any length of time, sit in a firm armchair and please, don't slouch!

Let the Fun Begin!

English or Continental? (No, it's not your choice of breakfast)

One of the biggest frustrations for a new knitter is finding the most comfortable way to hold the yarn and needles. With just a little time and patience, your hands will fall into a comfortable rhythm. This can be a bit confusing, mostly because no two people do it the same way. The two main styles of knitting are English and Continental. Though both create the same end product, most knitters have very specific opinions about which method is superior (theirs of course). Here's the major difference: English knitters hold and "throw" the yarn with their right hand, while Continental knitters manipulate the yarn with the left.

Once you've decided which hand will hold the working yarn, there's still one more decision to make—how to hold the needles. There is honestly no right or wrong way to accomplish this, so experiment with the different choices. You will soon develop your own unique style.

Be prepared for a little awkwardness in the beginning. Give yourself plenty of time to get comfortable with the new hand positions and motions involved in knitting. With a little time and patience, you'll soon have all of your friends in fancy new sweaters!

Casting On

There are many ways to get those initial stitches on the needle. We have selected two of the simplest, most sturdy, and neatly attractive versions to get you started. The first, a double cast-on, uses one needle and two lengths of yarn. The second method, the knit-on variation, uses two needles and one strand of yarn.

A solid cast-on leads to good results. The best way to perfect this method is to practice casting on until it becomes an easy process.

It's possible that when you first start to cast on, your foundation row will be so tight that it'll be tricky to get the needle through those little loops. If you have this problem, try casting on with two needles held together or use a needle two sizes larger than the one called for in the pattern. (Switch back to the correct needle size when you begin knitting.)

Slip Knot

The slip knot is the beginning of the cast-on process—it anchors the yarn to the needles and makes casting on possible. Before you begin the slip knot, decide which method of casting on to try. For the double cast-on method, leave about an inch of yarn for every stitch you want to place on the needle. If you choose the knit-on method, leave eight to ten inches between the end of the yarn and the slip knot.

Slip Knot

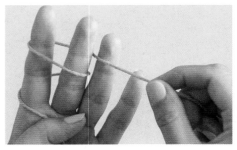

1 Hold the short end of the yarn in your palm with your thumb. Wrap the yarn twice around the index and middle fingers.

2 Pull the strand attached to the ball through the loop between your two fingers, forming a new loop.

3 Place the new loop on the needle. Tighten the loop on the needle by pulling on both ends of the yarn to form a slip knot. You are now ready to begin casting on.

Double Cast-On Slip Knot

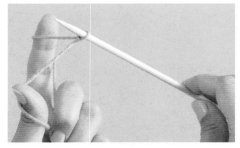

1 Make a slip knot on the right-hand needle, leaving a long tail. Wind the tail end around your left thumb, as shown. Wrap the yarn from the ball over your left index finger and secure the ends in your palm.

2 Insert the needle upward in the loop on your thumb.

3 With the needle, draw the yarn from the ball around your index finger through the loop to form a stitch. Take your thumb out of the loop and tighten the loop on the needle. Continue in this way until all the stitches are cast on.

Knit-On Cast-On

1 Make a slip knot on the left needle. *Insert the right needle from front to back into the stitch on the left needle. Wrap the yarn around the right needle as if to knit (see page 11).

2 Draw the yarn through the first stitch to make a new stitch, but do not drop the first stitch from the left needle.

3 Slip the new stitch to the left needle. Repeat from the * (in step 1) until the required number of stitches is cast on.

Knit Stitch

After you are comfortable with the cast-on, you can begin knitting. There are two different ways to make each knit stitch (English or Continental method). Which you use depends on your own comfort.

It may take some time to feel at ease, but keep working at it and it'll get easier. If you have any friends at yarn shops or knitting clubs, this is a good time to stay in touch. Being in contact with an experienced knitter will make the learning process easier.

Knit Stitch: English

1 Hold the needle with the cast-on stitches in your left hand. Hold the working needle in your right hand, wrapping the yarn around your fingers. Insert the right needle from front to back into the first cast-on stitch on the left needle. Keep the right needle under the left needle and the yarn at the back.

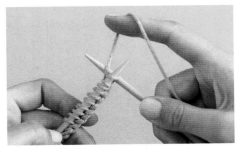

2 Wrap the yarn under and over the right needle.

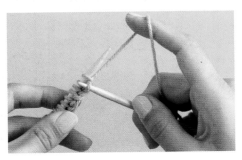

3 With the right needle, catch the yarn and pull it through the cast-on stitch.

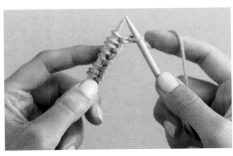

4 Slip the cast-on stitch off the left needle, leaving the newly formed stitch on the right needle. Repeat these steps in each subsequent stitch until all the stitches have been worked from the left needle. You have made one row of knit stitches.

Knit Stitch: Continental

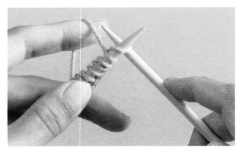

1 Hold the needles in the same way as the English method, but hold the yarn with your left hand rather than your right. Insert the right needle from front to back into the first cast-on stitch on the left needle. Keep the right needle under the left needle, with the yarn at the back.

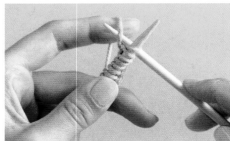

2 Lay the yarn over the right needle as shown.

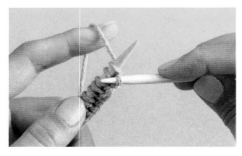

3 With the tip of the right needle, pull the strand through the cast-on stitch, holding the strand with the right index finger if necessary.

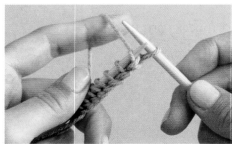

4 Slip the cast-on stitch off the left needle, leaving a newly formed stitch on the right needle. Continue to repeat these steps until you have worked all of the stitches from the left needle to the right needle. You have made one row of knit stitches.

Garter Stitch

The garter stitch is the simplest of all the stitch patterns and is completed by knitting every row. The end result is a flat, reversible, ridged fabric that will stand up well to wear and will not roll at the edges.

After you reach the end of the first row of knit stitches, move the full needle to your left hand and begin knitting each stitch all over again. Once you have completed several rows, you'll start to see the results. As you get deeper into the project, your growing strip of garter stitch will begin to look like a real piece of fabric.

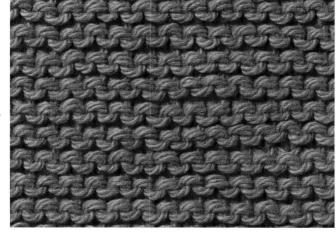

Purl Stitch

Take a breather and exercise those fingers. You will now learn an extremely important stitch in the world of knitting: the purl. Purling is just a backward version of knitting. When you put knitting and purling together, you can create literally hundreds of stitch patterns. Some people find the purl stitch more complicated than the knit stitch (which is why the knit stitch is taught first). Remember practice makes perfect. Once you understand how to purl, it will feel completely natural.

Purl Stitch: English

1 As with the knit stitch, hold the working needle in your right hand and the needle with the stitches in your left hand. The yarn is held and manipulated with your right hand and is kept to the front of the work. Insert the right needle from back to front into the first stitch on the left needle. The right needle is now in the front of the left needle, and the yarn is at the front of the work.

2 With your right index finger, wrap the yarn over and around the right needle.

3 Draw the right needle and the yarn backward through the stitch on the left needle, forming a loop on the right needle.

4 Slip the stitch off the left needle. You have made one purl stitch. Repeat these steps in each subsequent stitch until all stitches have been worked from the left needle. You have made one row of purl stitches.

Purl Stitch: Continental

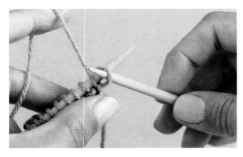

1 As with the knit stitch, hold the working needle in your right hand and the needle with the stitches in your left. The yarn is held and manipulated with your left hand and is kept to the front of the work. Insert the right needle from back to front into the first stitch on the left needle, keeping the yarn in front of the work.

2 Lay the yarn over the right needle as shown. Pull down on the yarn with your left index finger to keep the yarn taut.

3 Bring the right needle and the yarn backward through the stitch on the left needle, forming a loop on the right needle.

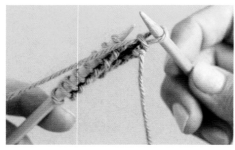

4 Slide the stitch off the left needle. Use your left index finger to tighten the new purl stitch on the right needle. Continue to repeat these steps until you have worked all of the stitches from the left needle to the right needle. You have made one row of purl stitches.

Stockinette Stitch

Knit and purl stitches can be combined to create the stockinette stitch, the beautiful V-patterned fabric that is most associateed with knitting. Simply alternate every row, working one row of knit stitches followed by one row of purl stitches.

Binding Off

After you are finished with your knitting, you will need to bind off your stitches so that your project will not unravel. Binding off is not complicated, but keep an eye on your tension. If you bind off too tightly, you will create a pucker on top. To prevent this, try binding off with a needle two sizes larger than the one used for the rest of the project.

Basic Knit Bind-Off

1 Knit two stitches. * Insert the left needle into the first stitch on the right needle.

2 Pull this stitch over the second stitch and off the right needle.

3 One stitch remains on the right needle as shown. Knit the next stitch. Repeat from the * (in step 1) until you have bound off the required number of stitches.

Joining Yarn

Soon enough, you will be knitting along and realize that your yarn ball is looking smaller and smaller. Don't panic—it's simply time to join a new ball of yarn.

Joining yarn works best at the end of a row. That way, it will be easier to weave in your ends without creating too much of a bulge. Simply tie the new yarn loosely around the old yarn, leaving at least a 6"(15cm) tail. Then untie the knot and weave in the ends.

To change yarn in the middle of a row, simply poke your right needle into the next stitch, wrap the new yarn around the needle in place of the old yarn, and keep on knitting. After you've reached the end of a row, tie the old and new strands together so that they don't unravel.

Weaving in Ends

When the time comes that you finish your project, you'll discover you have loose ends. In order to hide those strands and create a product that truly looks finished, you must weave the loose ends into the wrong side of the knitted fabric.

To begin, carefully untie the knot you made when first joining the new yarn. Take the loose strand and thread it through the yarn needle, snaking the needle (and attached yarn) down through approximately five of the free loops along the edge of your knitting. Remember to snip close to the work and remove whatever's left, but be careful not to cut the actual knitting. Then, thread the second strand through the needle and weave up.

If you need to change the yarn in the middle of a row, untie the knot and weave one loose piece in each direction horizontally, following the path of the affected stitch through five or six additional stitches on the wrong side of the work. You should always double-check the right side of the fabric to make sure no puckering or slackness has crept in.

Chapter Three
next steps

Beginner or no, there's more to knitting than baby steps

Once you have stitched scarves to your heart's content and made blankets for all of the babies among your friends and family, it's time to advance to shaping. These techniques are simple, and learning them will open you up to new horizons. Schematics, ribbing, and stitch gauges are also important. You're almost ready for the world of sweater making!

Less Is More: Decreasing

Decreasing (or reducing the number of stitches in a row) is a method of creating shaping within a knitting piece. Two of the easiest and most common decreases are the knit two together (k2tog) and purl two together (p2tog) decreases. These basic decreases slant to the right on the knit side of the work.

K2TOG: Insert the right needle from front to back (knitwise) into the next two stitches on the left needle. Wrap the yarn around the right needle (as when knitting) and pull it through. You have decreased one stitch.

P2TOG: Insert the right needle into the front loops (purlwise) of the next two stitches on the left needle. Wrap the yarn around the right needle (as when purling) and pull it through. You have decreased one stitch.

Increasing Opportunities

Increasing also changes the number of stitches. As with decreasing, there are various ways to do it. The bar increase, which is made by working in the front and back loops of the same stitch, is extremely common.

Knit Front and Back (kfb)

1 To increase on the knit side, insert the right needle knitwise into the stitch to be increased. Wrap the yarn around the right needle and pull it through as if knitting, but leave the stitch on the left needle.

2 Insert the right needle into the back of the same stitch. Wrap the yarn around the needle and pull it through. Slip the stitch off the left needle. You now have two stitches on the right needle.

Working in the Front and Back Loops

The loop closest to you is the front of the stitch. This is the loop you'll normally work into. To knit into the front loop, insert the right needle from left to right into the stitch on the left needle. To purl into the front loop, insert needle from right to left into the stitch.

To knit into the back loop (loop farthest from you), insert the right needle from right to left under left needle and into the stitch. To purl into the back loop, insert the needle from behind into the stitch.

Knitting into the back loop

Purling into the back loop

Take a Ribbing

The popular stockinette stitch is created by alternating rows of knit and purl stitches. However, it's also possible to switch back and forth within the same row to create many different patterns.

Ribbing is the most popular knit/purl combination. It is stretchy and has the ability to bounce back into place, making it ideal for hems, necks, and cuffs. In ribbing, you can make a total garment—ribbed sweaters create a slimming effect that any wearer would love. There'll be more about ribbing in Chapter 5.

Hint: For beginners, the trickiest part about ribbing is remembering to shift the yarn back and forth when working the different stitches. In knit 2, purl 2 ribbing, you knit two stitches, move the yarn between the two needles to the front of the work, and then purl two stitches. When you are ready to knit again, return the yarn to the back of the work by passing it between the two needles, then continue with your pattern. If the yarn isn't shifted from back to front and front to back between knit and purl stitches you will end up with extra stitches on your needle and a rectangular piece that will quickly become a triangle.

Basic Ribbing (Moving Yarn Back and Forth)

When knitting a stitch, as you've probably noticed by now, the yarn is always held at the back of the work. In purling however, the yarn is always at the front. With ribbing, when you move from a knit to a purl stitch you must be sure the yarn is in the correct position to work the next stitch. When you are moving the yarn from the back to the front, or vice versa, the yarn should go between the two needles, not over them.

Yarn in the back

Yarn in the front

Get in Gauge

The gauge swatch, the first step in garment making, is a square piece of knitted fabric that demonstrates how you, the needles, and the yarn interact before you get going on the main project. You will find a recommended gauge, or stitches and rows per inch, at the beginning of the instructions on every project, usually directly beneath the suggestions for yarn weight and needle size.

To create the gauge swatch, gather the exact yarn and needles that you plan to use for your project (even the smallest differences such as yarn color and needle brand can affect your gauge). Cast on a number of stitches that will give you more than four inches across, and then work in stockinette stitch or the specified stitch pattern until you have made a bit more than four vertical inches of fabric.

These two squares of knitting illustrate the importance of the gauge swatch. Each swatch is made with an identical number of stitches and rows, but the one on the left uses a smaller needle size than the one on the right. Are you inspired to make a gauge swatch before starting a whole garment? We hope so!

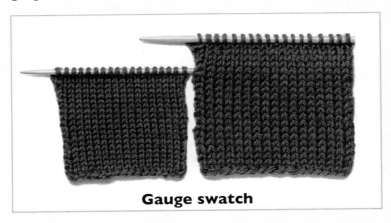

Gauge swatch

You can measure your gauge swatches with a tape measure or use a stitch gauge (see page 20) to count the stitches.

Remove the needle from the stitches (without binding off) and put the sample on a flat, smooth surface like a hardwood floor or kitchen table. Using a tape measure, ruler, or stitch gauge, measure across four inches (10 cm) of the knitting and count the number of stitches within those four inches (10 cm). If you have more stitches to the inch than the pattern calls for, go up one needle size. If you have fewer stitches than recommended, try again with a smaller needle. Next, check the number of rows in four inches (10 cm), too.

When you are as near as achievable to the recommended gauge, go ahead and begin knitting your garment, but don't forget about gauge in general just yet.

You can make the gauge swatch easier to work with by including selvage stitches on the edges of the square. Selvage stitches help the piece of fabric lay nice and flat, as well as making measuring easier, by giving you clear-cut edges between which to measure. To craft them, work two rows of garter stitch (knit every row) at the top and bottom of the swatch and include two stitches in garter stitch at the beginning and end of each stockinette row.

At times, the gauge of your actual garment may change dramatically from the gauge of your original swatch. After you've worked about 5 inches (12 cm) of the first piece of your project, recheck your gauge by laying the piece down on a flat surface and pulling out your tape measure (or stitch gauge) again. Your knitting should be as near to the suggested gauge as it was before. In the event that it's not, you'll have to unravel what you've done and start again using a different needle size. As you rip out the rows and roll the yarn back into a ball, remember it is better to do this now and have a usable garment in the long run.

Tip: Knitters believe that creating the gauge swatch is an extra, unnecessary step that can be skipped. This is not true. Always make the gauge swatch! Let's say your knitting is a half inch off of suggested gauge—your whole garment can end up unwearable! There's nothing quite as frustrating as working diligently on an adult's hat that ends up being the size of a toddler's, or making a baby's cap that would fit a grown man.

What on Earth Is a "Stitch Gauge"?

A stitch gauge is a flat rectangle of metal or plastic that simplifies the process of measuring gauge by providing a little window through which you can easily count stitches. First, lay your knitting down on a flat surface and then line up the L-shaped window with the corner of a stitch. Count the number of Vs in the window (both horizontally and vertically) to get accurate stitch and row gauges.

Some gauges also feature a row of holes that can be used to identify the size of unmarked needles. Slip the needle into the holes until you find one that lets the needle pass all the way through. The hole's corresponding number is your needle's size.

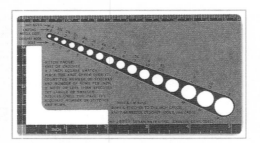

Keep It Short: Knitting Abbreviations

As you begin using knitting patterns, you will see that they seem to be written in a completely different language. For instance, what on earth does "*K1, p1; rep from *" mean? These confusing groups of letters, numbers, and symbols are part of a system of knitting terminology that saves space in patterns and makes instructions easier to read. The terms you'll run across in this book are listed on page 21.

Grasping Schematics

When you reach the end of most sweater patterns, you will find line drawings with bullets and numbers skirting the sides, and words like "Back" and "Left Front" scrawled across the centers. These are called schematics, and have some very important uses.

Schematics are drawn to scale. They give you an at-a-glance rundown of all the measurements, angles, and shapes of the sweater you're making. Schematics will reveal if the sweater tapers at the waist or narrows at the shoulders, and indicate the exact depth and width of the armholes, bust, and sleeves. They'll also provide you with a small idea of what your sweater pieces will look like when completed. **Hint:** Schematics will also be very useful for blocking (see Chapter 4).

When making a cardigan, the schematics are like those for a pullover sweater, but the front is different. One of the two front pieces will be drawn, and then you just have to visualize (or sketch) a mirror image for the other. That's not so hard, right?

Knitting Abbreviations

approx approximately

beg begin, beginning

ch I chain one (crochet loop)

cont continue

dec decrease

dpn double-pointed needle(s)

in/cm/mm inches/centimeters/millimeters

inc increase

inc (dec) sts evenly across row Count the number of stitches in the row, and then divide that number by the number of stitches to be increased (decreased). The result of this division will tell you how many stitches to work between each increased (decreased) stitch.

k knit

k the knit and p the purl sts This is a phrase used when a pattern of knit and purl stitches has been established and will be continued for some time. When the stitch that's facing you looks like a V, knit it. When it looks like a bump, purl it.

k2tog knit two together (a method of decreasing explained on page 17)

k3tog knit three together (worked same as k2tog, but insert needle into 3 sts instead of 2 for a double decrease)

knitwise Insert the needle into the stitch as if you were going to knit it.

M I With the needle tip, lift the strand between the last stitch knit and the next stitch on the left-hand needle and knit into the back of it. One knit stitch has been added.

oz/g ounces/grams (usually in reference to amount of yarn in a single ball)

p purl

p2tog purl two together (a method of decreasing explained on page 17)

pat pattern

pm place marker

purlwise Insert the needle into the stitch as if you were going to purl it.

rem remain, remains, or remaining

rep repeat

rep from * Repeat the instructions after the asterisk as many times as indicated. If the directions say "rep from * to end," continue to repeat the instructions after the asterisk to the end of the row.

reverse shaping A term used for garments like cardigans where shaping for the right and left fronts is identical, but reversed. For example, neck edge stitches decreased at the beginning of the row for the first piece will be decreased at the end of the row on the second. In general, follow the directions for the first piece, being sure to mirror the decreases (increases) on each side.

RS right side

SKP Slip one stitch to right-hand needle. Knit the next stitch and pass the slipped stitch over the knit stitch.

SK2P Slip one stitch, knit two stitches together, pass slipped stitch over the two stitches knit together.

sl st slip stitch

sl Transfer the indicated stitches from the left to the right needle without working (knitting or purling) them.

Small (Medium, Large) The most common method of displaying changes in pattern for different sizes. In general, the measurements, stitch counts, directions, etc. for the smallest size come first, followed by the increasingly larger sizes in parentheses. When there is only one number given, it applies to all of the sizes.

ssk slip one, slip one, knit slipped stitches together

St st stockinette stitch

st/sts stitch/stitches

work even Continue in the established pattern without working any increases or decreases.

WS wrong side

wyib with yarn in back

yo yarn over

Oops! A Quick-Fix Guide to Correcting Mistakes

As a knitter, you will make a mistake from time to time—we all do. Luckily fixing them is no big deal. Here are a few easy fixes for some of the most frequent errors that plague beginners as well as veterans.

Picking Up a Dropped Knit Stitch

Knit Side

1 This method is used when a knit stitch has been dropped on only one row. Work to where the stitch was dropped. Be sure that the loose strand is behind the dropped stitch.

2 Insert the right needle from front to back into the dropped stitch and under the loose horizontal strand behind it.

3 Insert the left needle from the back into the dropped stitch on the right needle, and pull this stitch over the loose strand.

4 Transfer this newly made stitch back to the left needle by inserting the left needle from front to back into the stitch and slipping it off the right needle.

Picking Up a Dropped Purl Stitch

Purl Side

1 This method is used when a purl stitch has been dropped only on one row. Work to the dropped purl stitch. Be sure that the loose horizontal strand is in front of the dropped stitch.

2 Insert the right needle from back to front into the dropped stitch, and then under the loose horizontal strand.

3 With the left needle, lift the dropped stitch over the horizontal strand and off the right needle.

4 Transfer the newly made purl stitch back to the left needle by inserting the left needle from front to back into the stitch and slipping it off the right needle.

Preventing an Extra Knit Stitch at the End of a Row

Knit Side

1 If you bring the yarn back over the top of the needle at the beginning of the knit row, the first stitch will have two loops instead of one, as shown.

2 To avoid creating this extra stitch, keep the yarn under the needle when taking it to the back to knit the first stitch.

Purl Side

1 At the beginning of a purl row, if the yarn is at the back, and then brought to the front under the needle, the first stitch will have two loops instead of one, as shown.

2 To avoid making these two loops, the yarn should be at the front before you purl the first stitch.

Chapter Four
a fine finish

Knitting requires that you tie up your loose ends.

Finishing your knits involves a few simple steps: blocking (shaping the pieces you've knit), sewing those pieces together, and weaving in all the loose ends. If you like you can add some lovely finishing touches, like buttonholes. Soon you'll be whipping out some very professional-looking sweaters. Dear knitters, you are entering the home stretch.

New Knits on the Block

Sometimes, the freshly-knit garment may appear wavy and misshapen. Luckily yarn is very forgiving. Colors and patterns may be more fun, but without blocking, even a perfectly knit garment won't look right. So, please, pull out that blocking equipment (see below) and follow along as we teach you how to mold your already-beautiful pieces into shape.

Wet and steam are the two main methods of blocking. The Pressing Guide (page 27) will aid you in discovering which type is best for your project. Before beginning either method, gather up any schematics or measurements from the pattern, and use them like architectural plans. With them, you will know exactly how far the pieces should stretch and where they should dip and swell.

What You'll Need:

1 Flat, covered, padded surface large enough to hold one piece of knitting (e.g., carpet or bed covered with plastic and a towel).

2 Rust-proof T-pins (AVOID pins with plastic heads—these will melt during steam blocking).

3 Tape measure.

4 Spray bottle with cool water or basin full of cool water (wet blocking) or steam iron or handheld steamer (steam blocking).

5 Towels (be sure they're colorfast).

6 Pressing cloth.

Pinning and Blocking

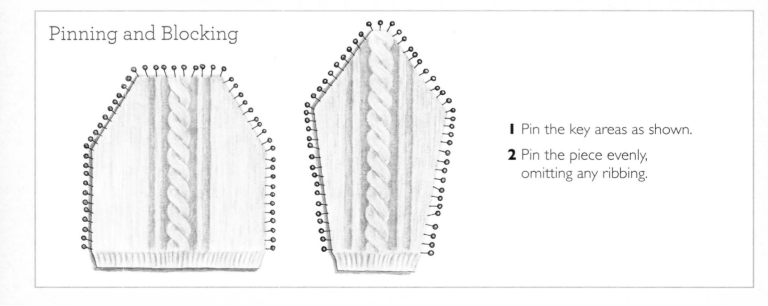

1 Pin the key areas as shown.

2 Pin the piece evenly, omitting any ribbing.

Wet Blocking

When wet blocking, either immerse the knitted pieces in cool water, squeeze them out, place them on the blocking surface, and stretch them to their exact measurements according to the schematics. Alternatively you can pin the pieces first and then wet them down with a water-filled spray bottle. Your personal preference will dictate the method you use, though you may find the spraying method to be a bit less awkward. Once the pieces are pinned and wet, walk away and don't bother them until they are completely dry. This may take 24 hours or more, so be patient.

Steam Blocking

For steam blocking, first pin the pieces on a flat surface according to the schematics. Then fire up your steam iron or hand-held steamer, and steam the pieces until the fabric is convincingly damp. It is important that you never touch the iron to the stitches. If you must press, do so lightly and protect your knitted investment by placing a colorfast towel or pressing cloth between the fabric and the hot metal. As with wet blocking, leave the pieces to dry. Drying time after steaming probably won't take as long as it does for wet blocking, but you may still need to be patient for several hours. While waiting, you can plan your next sweater!

Pressing Guide

Different fibers will react differently to heat, so it is best to know what to expect before you press or steam them. Try to remember that many yarns are combinations of fibers. Choose the process that is best suited to all the components of your yarn. If you are unsure about fiber content, test your gauge swatch before blocking your sweater pieces.

Angora Wet block by spraying.

Linen Wet block or warm/hot steam press.

Mohair Wet block by spraying.

Synthetics Carefully follow instructions on ball band—usually wet block by spraying. Do not press.

Wool and all wool-like fibers (alpaca, camel hair, cashmere) Wet block by spraying or warm steam press.

Wool blends Wet block by spraying; do not press unless tested.

Cotton Wet block or warm/hot steam press.

Lurex Do not block.

Novelties Do not block.

Seams Like a Dream

After the last strand of every piece of your garment has been finished, there's one thing left to do in order to make your pieces wearable: sew them together. Sewing together, or "seaming," is achieved with a yarn needle and the same yarn you used to make your project.

Sewing together knitted fabric can be done in many different ways, with each method serving a different purpose. One kind of seaming will be best to join adjacent lengths of stockinette stitch, but another is better to connect vertical and horizontal pieces of the same fabric. Pattern instructions will usually recommend a particular method to use, so just follow the directions, and your product will come out beautifully.

Make sure you have correctly lined up those little stitches before sewing those seams. This is done by finding the cast-on stitches on both sides. Pin the stitches together with a straight pin or safety pin. After that, count up ten rows on each side and pin the corresponding stitches together. Keep at it until you get to the top of the two pieces.

When creating a garment that is worked all in one piece, like a hat, the rows should line up exactly. If you end up with extra rows on one side at the top, go back and see where stragglers have lagged behind on the opposite side. If you are seaming two separate pieces, you may have to ease in extra rows if one piece turned out to be slightly longer than the other.

How to Begin Seaming

If there is a long tail left from your cast-on row, this strand can be used to begin sewing. To make a neat join at the lower edge with no gap, use the technique shown here.

Thread the strand into a yarn needle. With the right sides of both pieces facing you, insert the yarn needle from back to front into the corner stitch of the piece without the tail. Making a figure eight with the yarn, insert the needle from back to front into the stitch with the cast-on tail. Tighten to close the gap.

Vertical Seam on Stockinette Stitch

The vertical seam is worked from the right side and is used to join two edges row by row. It hides the uneven stitches at the edge of a row and creates an invisible seam, making it appear that the knitting is continuous.

Insert the yarn needle under horizontal bar or two, one-half stitch in from the edge on one side. Insert the needle into corresponding bar or bars on the other piece. Continue alternating from side to side.

Vertical Seam on Garter Stitch

This seam joins two edges row by row similar to vertical seaming on stockinette stitch. The alternating pattern of catching top and bottom loops of the stitches makes it so that only you can tell there's a join.

Insert the yarn needle into the top loop on one side, then in the bottom loop of the corresponding stitch on the other side. Continue to alternate in this way.

Horizontal Seam on Stockinette Stitch

This seam is used to join two bound-off edges, such as for shoulder seams or hoods, and is worked stitch by stitch. You must have the same number of stitches on each piece so that the finished seam will resemble a continuous row of knit stitches. Be sure to pull the yarn tightly enough to hide the bound-off edges.

With the bound-off edges together, lined up stitch for stitch, insert the yarn needle under a stitch inside the bound-off edge of one side and then under the corresponding stitch on the other side. Repeat all the way across the join.

Vertical to Horizontal Seam

Used to connect a bound-off edge to a vertical length of knitted fabric, this seam requires careful pre-measuring and marking to ensure an even seam.

Insert the yarn needle under a stitch inside the bound-off edge of the vertical piece. Insert the needle under one or two horizontal bars between the first and second stitches of the horizontal piece. Shown here on Stockinette stitch.

Pick-Up Lines

Sometimes you will need to "pick up stitches." While this phrase might sound like a children's game, once you get the hang of it, it's as easy as pie. Picking up stitches means that with a knitting needle or crochet hook and a new strand of yarn, you dip into and out of the edge of the knitted fabric, creating new loops. These new loops will serve as the foundation for a collar, button band, sleeve, or baby bootie instep.

Two important things to focus on for picking up stitches along a straight edge are the two Ss: side and spacing. For the first "S," be sure to start picking up stitches with the right side facing you. The second "S" reminds you to space the stitches evenly along the fabric. Always make sure that the picked-up loops aren't clustered together or separated by vast expanses along the edge.

Picking Up Along a Bound-off Edge	Picking Up Along a Side Edge

1 Insert the knitting needle into the top stitich, just under the bind-off. Wrap the yarn around the needle knitwise. **2** Draw the yarn through. You have picked up one stitch. Continue to pick up a stitch in each column of knits under the bind-off.	**1** Insert the knitting needle into the corner stitch of the first row, one stitch in from the side edge. Wrap the yarn around the needle knitwise. **2** Draw the yarn through. You have picked up one stitch. Continue to pick up stitches along the edge. Occasionally skip one row to keep the edge from flaring.

Picking Up Shaped Edges

When picking up stitches for a sloped edge (such as for a neck), take just a little more care than for a straight edge. Much of this effort comes in the spacing. It's especially important that the stitches be picked up evenly when you are making a neck band, so the band will not flare out (too many stitches picked up) or pull in (too few stitches picked up).

The Hole Truth

Have you ever looked at perfectly created buttonholes in cardigans and wondered how the knitter made them? We are about to teach you how, so you too can enjoy creating this form of perfection. We will study the two-row horizontal buttonhole, the one-row horizontal buttonhole, and the yarn over buttonhole. The two-row and one-row buttonholes are shown worked over four stitches, though you might need to use more or fewer depending on the size of your button.

Two-Row Horizontal Buttonhole

The most common buttonhole is the two-row horizontal buttonhole, probably because it is adaptable to be smaller or larger depending on the size of your button. It is made by binding off a number of stitches on one row and casting them on again on the next. The last stitch bound off is part of the left side of the buttonhole.

1 On the first row, work to the location of the buttonhole. Knit two. With the left needle, pull one stitch over the other stitch, *knit one, pull the second stitch over the knit one; repeat from the * twice more. Four stitches have been bound off.

2 On the next row, work to the bound-off stitches and cast on four stitches. On the next row, work these stitches through the back loops to tighten them.

One-Row Horizontal Buttonhole

The one-row horizontal buttonhole is the neatest buttonhole and requires no further reinforcing. Although it's slightly more complicated to work than the two-row horizontal buttonhole, the extra effort produces a fantastic, super-clean result.

1 Work to the buttonhole, bring yarn to front, and slip a stitch purlwise. Place yarn at back and leave it there. *Slip next stitch from left needle. Pass the first slipped stitch over it; repeat from the * three times more (not moving yarn). Slip the last bound-off stitch to the left needle and turn work.

2 Using the cable cast-on with the yarn at the back, cast on five stitches as follows: *Insert the right needle between the first and second stitches on the left needle, draw up a loop, place the loop on the left needle; repeat from the * four times more, turn work.

3 Slip the first stitch with the yarn in back from the left needle and pass the extra cast-on stitch over it to close the buttonhole. Work to the end of the row.

Yarn-Over Buttonhole

If you are creating a smaller or children's garment, the yarn over buttonhole might be your best bet. It produces an especially small space in the fabric. To create this buttonhole, knit two stitches together, followed by a yarn over. On the return row, work the yarn over as if it is a stitch.

Work to the location of the buttonhole. Bring the yarn from the back of the work to the front between the two needles. Knit the next stitch, bringing the yarn to the back over the needle as shown.

Tip: Not sure how many buttons you need? It's always best to have space for more. The smaller the gaps between buttons, the flatter and smoother your cardigan band will appear. It's also good to buy the buttons for your project before you start knitting so that you'll have an idea of the size, spacing, and number of buttonholes on the buttonhole band.

Buttonhole Spacing

The goal is to have your buttonholes spaced as evenly as possible. Accomplish this by placing markers on the button band for the first and last buttonholes. Measure the distance between them and place markers evenly for the remaining buttonholes.

Ensure your buttons and buttonholes line up in the end by counting: the number of rows between the lower edge and the first marker, between the first and second markers, and so on. Make a note of how many rows separate each marker, and then make your buttonholes on the corresponding rows of the buttonhole band.

Tip: Many patterns will suggest the button and buttonhole bands to be worked separately and sewn on later. However, on some styles you can work the front bands with the main piece. This will save time and eliminate the need for extra seaming. This technique also allows you to space the buttonholes precisely along the edge of the sweater.

Button Up

When you are ready to sew on the buttons, you can use yarn (if it goes through the button) or matching thread. With metal buttons, which may cut the thread, you may wish to use waxed dental floss. Double the thread and tie a knot on the end. Then slip your button onto the needle and thread. You can further secure the button with a square of fabric or felt at the back, which is especially desirable on garments that receive heavy wear, such as jackets.

Chapter Five:
a basic stitch sampler

Some people are content sticking with stockinette, but chances are, once you've grown confident with the basics, you'll want to go beyond the garter, so to speak.

There are two ways to attain interest in knitted fabrics—color and texture. The yarns you choose can have amazing results, but you already know that. At this point, you can add colorwork and stitchwork to the equation for a beautiful outcome. This is when your project becomes a lot more interesting.

Add Some Texture

It's time to revisit ribbing. Remember when we alternated knits and purls within a row to create nice stretchy ribs? This stretchy quality makes ribbing the preferred stitch for sweater cuffs and hems. Ribbed fabrics are reversible, which makes ribbing perfect for scarves. In addition to several variations on the ribbing theme, there are myriad other easy ways of combining stitches to create texture in a knitted fabric, many of which simply involve alternating stitches within a row.

Ribbing

You can knit a ribbing in just about any combination of knits and purls and even twist the stitches to get different effects.

Twisted K1, P1 (half twist)

(Over an odd number of stitches)
Row 1 (RS) K1 through the back loop, *p1, k1 through the back loop; repeat from * to end.
Row 2 P1, *k1, p1; repeat from * to end.
Repeat rows 1 and 2.

Twisted K1, P1 (full twist)

(Over an odd number of stitches)
Row 1 (RS) K1 through the back loop, *p1, k1 through the back loop; repeat from * to end.
Row 2 P1 through the back loop, *k1, p1 through the back loop; repeat from * to end.
Repeat rows 1 and 2.

K5, P2

(multiple of 7 stitches plus 2 extra)
Row 1 (WS) K2, *p5, k2; repeat from * to end.
Row 2 P2, *k5, p2; repeat from * to end.
Repeat rows 1 and 2.

K2, P5

(multiple of 7 stitches plus 2 extra)
Row 1 (RS) K2, *p5, k2; repeat from * to end.
Row 2 P2, *k5, p2; repeat from * to end.
Repeat rows 1 and 2.

.

Basic Textures

It might be some time before you are ready to reel yourself into an entire Irish fisherman's sweater, each one unique in its intricate texture. You'll be pleasantly surprised, however, to discover that some of the prettiest textured stitches are the easiest to knit. The beautiful seed stitch, for example, requires a simple knit one, purl one, and alternates on the next row with purl one, knit one (see below). How lovely would it be to create a patchwork blanket of swatches—made up of all the new stitches you are learning!

Seed Stitch
(over an even number of stitches)
Row 1 (RS) *K1, p1; rep from * to end.
Row 2 *P1, k1; rep from * to end.
Rep rows 1 and 2.

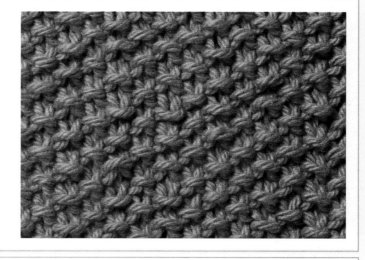

Moss Stitch
(over an odd number of stitches)
Rows 1 and 3 (RS) Knit.
Row 2 P1, *k1, p1; rep from * to end.
Row 4 K1, *p1; k1; rep from * to end.
Rep rows 1–4.

Horizontal Dash Stitch
(multiple of 10 stitches plus 6)
Row 1 (RS) P6, *k4, p6; rep from * to end.
Row 2 and all WS rows Purl.
Row 3 Knit.
Row 5 P1, *k4, p6; rep from *, end last rep p1.
Row 7 Knit.
Row 8 Purl.
Rep rows 1–8.

Basketweave

(multiple of 8 stitches plus 5)
Row 1 (RS) Knit.
Row 2 K5, *p3, k5; rep from * to end.
Row 3 P5, *k3, p5; rep from * to end.
Row 4 Rep row 2.
Row 5 Knit.
Row 6 K1, *p3, k5; rep from *, end last rep k1.
Row 7 P1, *k3, p5; rep from *, end last rep p1.
Row 8 Rep row 6.
Rep rows 1–8.

Embossed Diamonds

(multiple of 10 stitches plus 3)
Row 1 (RS) P1, k1, p1, *[k3, p1] twice, k1, p1;
rep from * to end.
Row 2 P1, k1, *p3, k1, p1, k1, p3, k1; rep from *, end p1.
Row 3 K4, *[p1, k1] twice, p1, k5; rep from *,
end last rep k4.
Row 4 P3, *[k1, p1] 3 times, k1, p3; rep from * to end.
Row 5 Rep row 3.
Row 6 Rep row 2.
Row 7 Rep row 1.
Row 8 P1, k1, p1, *k1, p5, [k1, p1] twice;
rep from * to end.
Row 9 [P1, k1] twice, *p1, k3, [p1, k1] 3 times;
rep from *, end last rep [p1,k1] twice, p1.
Row 10 Rep row 8.
Rep rows 1–10.

Peppercorn Stitch

(multiple of 4 stitches plus 3)
Peppercorn st K next st, [sl st just knit back to LH
needle and knit it again tbl] 3 times.
Row 1 (RS) K3, *peppercorn st, k3; rep from * to end.
Row 2 Purl.
Row 3 K1, *peppercorn st, k3; rep from *, end
last rep k1.
Row 4 Purl.
Rep rows 1–4.

Bramble/Blackberry Stitch

(multiple of 4 stitches)

Row 1 (RS) Purl.

Row 2 *[K1, p1, k1] in same st, p3tog; rep from * to end.

Row 3 Purl.

Row 4 *P3tog, [k1, p1, k1] in same st; rep from * to end.

Rep rows 1–4.

Dot-Knot Stitch

(multiple of 6 stitches plus 1)

Dot-not Stitch Insert RH needle from front to back under the horizontal strand between the first and second stitchess on left-hand needle, wrap yarn and draw through a loop loosely; insert the RH needle between same stitches above the horizontal strand, draw through another loop loosely; bring yarn to front between needles and purl the first stitch on the left-hand needle; with point of left-hand needle, pass the first loop over the second loop and the purled stitch and off needle; pass the second loop over the purled stitch and off the needle.

Row 1 (RS) Knit.

Row 2 and all WS rows Purl.

Row 3 K3, *work dot-knot stitch, k5; rep from *, end last rep k3.

Row 5 Knit.

Row 7 *Work dot-knot st, k5; rep from *, end k1.

Row 8 Purl.

Rep rows 1–8.

Hole Knitting!

Think back to earlier in this book when we went over buttonholes. This same yarn-over technique can be used to make gorgeous lace! It's rare that you will have a reason to knit lingerie, but it's easy to learn how to knit simple eyelet trims and inserts once you become accustomed to having holes in your knitting. As with colorwork knitting, most openwork stitches are charted out—perfect for those of us with a short attention span!

Basic Openwork Stitches

Eyelet Rows

(multiple of 2 stitches plus 2)

Rows 1, 5, 7, 9, 13 and 15 (RS) Knit.
Row 2 and all WS rows Purl.
Row 3 K1, *yo, SKP; rep from *, end k1.
Row 11 K1, *SKP, yo; rep from *, end k1.
Row 16 Knit.
Rep rows 1–16.

Open Leaves

(multiple of 12 stitches plus 1)

Row 1 (RS) K1, *k3, k2tog, yo, k1, yo, SKP, k4; rep from * to end.
Row 2 and all WS rows Purl.
Row 3 K1, *k2, k2tog, [k1, yo] twice, k1, SKP, k3; rep from * to end.
Row 5 K1, *k1, k2tog, k2, yo, k1, yo, k2, SKP, k2; rep from * to end.
Row 7 K1, *k2tog, k3, yo, k1, yo, k3, SKP, k1; rep from * to end.
Row 9 Knit.
Row 11 K1, *yo, SKP, k7, k2tog, yo, k1; rep from * to end.
Row 13 K1, *yo, k1, SKP, k5, k2tog, k1, yo, k1; rep from * to end.
Row 15 K1, *yo, k2, SKP, k3, k2tog, k2, yo, k1; rep from * to end.
Row 17 K1, *yo, k3, SKP, k1, k2tog, k3, yo, k1; rep from * to end.
Row 19 Knit.
Row 20 Purl.
Rep rows 1–20.

Chevron Eyelets

(multiple of 9 stitches)

Row 1 (RS) *K4, yo, SKP, k3; rep from * to end.
Row 2 and all WS rows Purl.
Row 3 *K2, k2tog, yo, k1, yo, SKP, k2; rep from * to end.
Row 5 *K1, k2tog, yo, k3, yo, SKP, k1; rep from * to end.
Row 7 *K2tog, yo, k5, yo, SKP; rep from * to end.
Row 8 Purl.
Rep rows 1–8.

Simple Vine

(multiple of 11 stitches plus 1)

Row 1 (RS) K2tog, *k5, yo, k1, yo, k2, sl 1, k2tog, psso;
rep from *, end last rep ssk.
Row 2 and all WS rows Purl.
Row 3 K2tog, *k4, yo, k3, yo, k1, sl 1, k2tog, psso; rep
from *, end last rep ssk.
Row 5 K2tog, *k3, yo, k5, yo, sl 1, k2tog, psso;
rep from *, end last rep ssk.
Row 7 K2tog, *k2, yo, k1, yo, k5, sl 1, k2tog, psso;
rep from *, end last rep ssk.
Row 9 K2tog, *k1, yo, k3, yo, k4, sl 1, k2tog, psso;
rep from *, end last rep ssk.
Row 11 K2tog, *yo, k5, yo, k3, sl 1, k2tog, psso;
rep from *, end last rep ssk.
Row 12 Rep row 2.
Rep rows 1–12.

Basic Cable

As with anything worthwhile, knitting involves practice, practice, practice. After all the work you've done, you are probably ready to give some basic cables a try. To do this, you will need small, double-pointed needles called cable needles. These work as placeholders for the stitches you'll need to come back to. By knitting "out of order," you can create an intriguing twisted effect. This concept can't truly be understood until you give it a try. Most cables are worked as knit stitches over a purl background, and many come with a chart. First test the waters with a mock cable that does not require a cable needle, then take the leap with a giant cable.

Simple Mock Cable

(multiple of 4 stitches plus 2)

2-st right twist (RT) K2tog leaving both sts on needle; insert RH needle into first st and k first st again; then sl both sts from needle.

Row 1 P2, *k2, p2; rep from * to end.

Rows 2 and 4 K2, *p2, k2; rep from * to end.

Row 3 P2, *RT, p2; rep from * to end.

Rep rows 1–4.

Giant Cable

Right cable

(panel of 16 stitches)

12-st right cable Sl 6 sts to cn and hold to back of work, k6, k6 from cn.

Rows 1 and 3 (RS) P2, k12, p2.

Row 2 and all WS rows K the knit sts and p the purl sts.

Row 5 P2, 12-st right cable, p2.

Row 7 Rep row 1.

Row 8 Rep row 2.

Rep rows 1–8.

Left cable

(panel of 16 stitches)

12-st left cable Sl 6 sts to cn and hold to front of work, k6, k6 from cn.

Rows 1 and 3 (RS) P2, k12, p2.

Row 2 and all WS rows K the knit sts and p the purl sts.

Row 5 P2, 12-st left cable, p2.

Row 7 Rep row 1.

Row 8 Rep row 2.

Rep rows 1–8.

Color My World

"For me, it's all about color. Color is magic," says knitting legend Kaffe Fassett, a master colorwork knitter. Fassett originally discovered yarn while visiting Scotland and went on to learn to knit while on the train ride back to London. "Since then," he says, "I've painted with yarn."

The easiest method of changing colors is simply to knit horizontal stripes. All you need to do is change colors at the ends of rows, carrying the unused color along the edge of your knitting. This technique is a favorite among neophyte knitters who are eager to delve into the wonderful world of using multiple hues of yarns but are still timid about attempting anything too complicated. It's true enough that you could change colors countless times and not run out of new shades, considering the myriad colors constantly available.

When you want to move on from stripes, remember that when dealing with colorwork, you must do whatever you can to keep your yarns from becoming twisted. With just two colors, it's easy—keep one color to your right and one to your left. It gets a little more complicated when you use several colors at the same time, but we aren't ready to talk about that just yet.

Simply Fair Isle

Who hasn't seen a lovely Fair Isle sweater and wanted one for her very own? Despite its intricate appearance, Fair Isle knitting usually calls for only two colors of yarn in each row (so you can hold one color in each hand) and no more than five to seven consecutive stitches in any one color. Each color has a symbol, and patterns are clearly charted on graph paper. It's not as complicated as it may look.

Intarsia

Is it your heart's desire to adorn your bedroom with heart pillows, or maybe a special Halloween pumpkin sweater for your grandson? For isolated blocks or shapes, learning intarsia is necessary. As with Fair Isle, you'll be using two balls of yarn, but this time you can knit big shapes with the second color. This is also known as "picture knitting." After you've mastered this fun technique, you can create all kinds of cool things for friends and family.

Perfecting Pop-Ups

Raised stitches such as knots and popcorns seem to appeal to kids of all ages. This is a great way to add texture to children's and baby garments. When knitting a raised stitch, you'll be increasing several stitches in one stitch and knitting a little ball that sticks up on the surface of your knitting. Knots are made by forming little loops on the front of the knitting. Raised stitches can be placed randomly or in a regular pattern to create overall texture.

Chapter Six
fun patterns

As soon as you learn the knit stitch, you are ready to start making your own garments. Here are 15 patterns to try at home. Start with an easy scarf, progress your way to a more challenging garment.

Yin Scarf

A scarf is a great first project, giving you a chance to show off your new knitting skills.

Knitted Measurements
• Approx 4" x 62"/10 x 157.5cm

Materials
• 6oz/170g, 250yd/230m of any worsted weight chenille yarn in red
• One pair size 9 (5.5mm) needles *or size to obtain gauge*

Gauge
14 sts and 28 rows to 4"/10cm over garter st using size 9 (5.5mm) needles.
Take time to check gauge.

Scarf
Cast on 14 sts. Work even in garter st (knit every row) until piece measures 62"/157.5cm from beg. Bind off. ■

Yin and Yang Scarf

If you're up to the challenge of a two-color project, make the Yin and Yang scarf.

Knitted Measurements
• Approx 7" x 60"/17.5 x 152.5cm

Materials
• 3oz/90g, 130yd/120m of any worsted weight chenille yarn each in black and blue
• One pair size 9 (5.5mm) needles *or size to obtain gauge*

Gauge
14 sts and 28 rows to 4"/10cm over garter st using size 9 (5.5mm) needles.
Take time to check gauge.

Note
When changing colors for yin and yang scarf, pick up new color from under dropped color to prevent holes.

Scarf
With A, cast on 12 sts, then with B, cast on 12 sts.
Row 1 (WS) With B, k12, with A, k12.
Row 2 With A, k12, with B, k12. Rep these 2 rows until piece measures 60"/152.5cm from beg. Bind off. ■

His and Hers Hats

Knit flat with a back seam, these classic watch caps work up fast in a super-bulky wool blend. The crown decreases neatly disappear into the ever-narrowing ribbing.

Sizes

Instructions are written for size Small/Medium. Changes for Medium/Large are in parentheses.

Knitted Measurements

- Head circumference 21¾ (24¾)"/55 (63)cm

Materials 5

- 1 ball in #180 Evergreen (His) or 1 ball in #130 Grass (Hers) of Wool-Ease Chunky by Lion Brand, 5oz/140g balls, each approx 153yd/140m (acrylic/wool)
- One pair size 11 (8mm) needles *or size to obtain gauge*
- Stitch markers

Gauge

8 sts and 11 rows to 3"/7.5cm over rib pat using size 11 (8mm) needles. *Take time to check gauge.*

Rib Pattern

(multiple of 8 sts)

Row 1 (RS) *K4, p4; rep from * to end. Rep row 1 for rib pat.

Hat

Cast on 58 (66) sts.

Next row (RS) K1 (selvage st), place st marker, work in rib pat across next 56 (64) sts, place st marker, k1 (selvage st). Keeping 1 st each side in garter st (k every row), cont to work rem sts in rib pat. Work even until piece measures 6"/15cm from beg, end with a WS row.

Crown shaping

Row 1 (RS) K1 (selvage st), *k1, k2tog, k1, p1, p2tog, p1; rep from *, end k1 (selvage st)—44 (50) sts.

Row 2 K1 (selvage st), *k3, p3; rep from *, end k1 (selvage st).

Row 3 K1 (selvage st), *k2tog, k1, p2tog, p1; rep from *, end k1 (selvage st)—30 (34) sts.

Row 4 K1 (selvage st), *k2, p2; rep from *, end k1 (selvage st).

Row 5 K1 (selvage st), *k2, p2tog; rep from *, end k1 (selvage st)—23 (26) sts.

Row 6 K1 (selvage st), drop marker, *k1, p2tog; rep from *, end drop marker, k1 (selvage st)—16 (18) sts.

Row 7 [K2tog] 8 (9) times—8 (9) sts. Cut yarn leaving a long tail. Thread tail in tapestry needle and weave through rem sts. Pull tight to gather, fasten off securely, then sew back seam. ■

Trellis Shawl

This rich wrap shawl (named for the elegant novelty yarn it's stitched in) provides quick-knit glamour for all skill levels. No finishing required—bind off, put it on, and go.

Knitted Measurements
Approx 18" x 60"/45.5 x 152.5cm

Materials **5**
• 10½oz/300g, 690yd/640m of any bulky weight ribbon yarn in blue multi
• Size 13 (9mm) circular needle, 36"/91.5cm long *or size to obtain gauge*

Gauge
15 sts and 20 rows to 4"/10cm over St st using size 13 (9mm) needle.
Take time to check gauge.

Note
A circular needle is used to accommodate the large number of stitches.

Shawl
Cast on 225 sts. Do not join. Work back and forth in St st (knit one row, purl one row) until piece measures 18"/45.5cm from beg, end with a RS row. Bind off all sts knitwise. ■

Mohair Poncho

**Simple garter stitch is all you need to create this cozy poncho.
Sew up the panels, add a pretty ribbon, and you're good to go.**

Sizes
Instructions are written for one size.

Knitted Measurements
Each piece measures approx 18" x 33"/45.5 x 84cm

Materials
- 7oz/200g, 330yd/310m of any bulky weight mohair blend yarn in green
- One pair size 11 (8mm) needles *or size to obtain gauge*
- 32"/81cm length of 1½"/38mm-wide ribbon
- Matching sewing thread
- Sewing needle

Gauge
12 sts and 20 rows to 4"/10cm over garter st using size 11 (8mm) needles.
Take time to check gauge.

Note
Poncho is made of two rectangular pieces that are sewn to each other leaving a neck opening (see assembly diagram).

Poncho
(make 2 pieces)
Cast on 54 sts. Work even in garter st until piece measures 33"/84cm from beg. Bind off.

Finishing
Referring to assembly diagram, use yarn to sew cast-on edge of first piece to left-hand edge of second piece, matching points A and B. Sew bound-off edge of second piece to right-hand edge of first piece matching points C and D. Using yarn, sew a gathering thread along A/B seam. Pull to gather; fasten off securely. Tie ribbon into a bow. Sew bow in place using sewing thread as pictured. ■

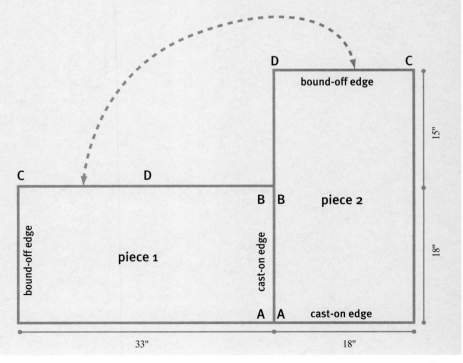

Baby Blanket

Weave your best wishes for baby into a lush, cashmere-blend blanket. The classic basketweave pattern is bordered on all sides by pretty seed stitch, which forms a self-finished edge.

Knitted Measurements
Approx 24½" x 27½"/ 62 x 70cm

Materials 4
- 7 balls in #101 Blossom of Superwash Merino Cashmere by Lion Brand, 1½oz/40g balls, each approx 87yd/80m (wool/nylon/cashmere)
- One pair size 8 (5mm) needles *or size to obtain gauge*
- Stitch markers

Gauge
19 sts and 32 rows to 4"/10cm over basketweave pat using size 8 (5mm) needles.
Take time to check gauge.

Seed Stitch
(multiple of 2 sts)
Row 1 (RS) *K1, p1; rep from * to end.
Row 2 K the purl sts and p the knit sts.
Rep Row 2 for Seed St.

Basketweave Pattern
(multiple of 8 sts plus 2)
Row 1 (WS) Purl.
Row 2 K2, *p6, k2; rep from * to end.
Row 3 P2, *k6, p2; rep from * to end.
Row 4 Rep row 2.
Row 5 Purl.
Row 6 P4, *k2, p6; rep from *, end k2, p4.
Row 7 K4, *p2, k6; rep from *, end p2, k4.
Row 8 Rep row 6.
Rep rows 1–8 for basketweave pat.

Blanket
Beg at bottom border, cast on 116 sts. Do not join. Work back and forth in seed st for 2"/5cm.

Beg pats
Next row (WS) Work in seed st across first 9 sts, place st marker, work row 1 of basketweave pat across next 98 sts, place st marker, work in seed st across last 9 sts. Keeping 9 sts each side in seed st for side borders, work center 98 sts in basketweave pat and work even until piece measures 25½"/64.5cm from beg, end with row 5.
Next row (RS) Work in seed st across all sts dropping markers. Cont in seed st until top border measures 2"/5cm. Bind off in seed st. ■

Chevron Afghan

This afghan will provide relaxation during and after its creation. Master the easy chevron pattern, and your knitting will develop a soothing rhythm. Finish the afghan and curl up with it for a well-deserved nap.

Knitted Measurements
Approx 42" x 57"/106.5 x 144.5cm

Materials 🝮 🝯
- 6oz/170g, 190yd/180m of any bulky weight textured acrylic yarn each in dark green (A), green and orange multi (B), and light brown (K)
- 3oz/90g, 140yd/130m of any bulky weight fuzzy acrylic yarn each in medium brown (C), and medium green (G)
- 1¾oz/50g, 60yd/60m of any super bulky weight wool blend yarn each in light brown, pink, yellow and blue multi (F), and dark brown, pink, yellow and blue multi (F)
- 1¾oz/50g, 90yd/90m of any bulky weight mohair blend yarn each in green, red, blue and yellow multi (D) and medium brown multi (J)
- 2½oz/70g, 60yd/60m of any super bulky weight textured acrylic blend yarn in lime green (H)
- 3oz/90g, 130yd/120m of any bulky weight chenille yarn each in medium brown (E) and medium green (M)
- 3oz/90g, 120yd/110m of any bulky weight chenille yarn in pink, red and purple multi (I)
- Size 11 (8mm) circular needle, 36"/91.5cm long *or size to obtain gauge*
- Stitch markers

Gauge
12 sts and 14 rows to 4"/10cm over pat st using a size 11 (8mm) needle.
Take time to check gauge.

Note
A circular needle is used to accommodate the large number of stitches.

Chevron Pattern
(multiple of 13 sts plus 2)
Row 1 (RS) Purl.
Row 2 Knit.
Row 3 K2, *yo, k4, SK2P, k4, yo, k2; rep from * to end.

Row 4 Purl.
Row 5 Rep row 3.
Row 6 Purl.
Row 7 Rep row 3.
Row 8 Purl.
Row 9 Rep row 3.
Row 10 Purl.
Rep rows 1–10 for chevron pat.

Afghan
With A, cast on 123 sts. Do not join.
Next row (RS) K2, place st marker, p center 119 sts, place st marker, k2.

Next row Knit.
Keeping 2 sts each side in garter st (k every row) for side borders, cont in chevron pat and stripe sequence on center 19 sts as folls: Work 10 rows each A, B, C, D, E, F, G, H, I, J, K, L, M, H, C, D, F, G, K, and B. Using B, work rows 1 and 2 twice more. Bind off. ■

Easy Pullover

This pullover makes a great "first sweater." Minimal shaping and chunky yarn will have you knitting it up in no time.

Sizes

Instructions are written for size Small. Changes for Medium, Large, and X-Large are in parentheses.

Knitted Measurements

Bust 35 (39, 43, 47)"/89 (99, 109, 119)cm
Length 22½ (23, 23½, 24½)"/57 (58.5, 59.5, 62) cm
Upper arm 13 (14, 15,16)"/33 (35.5, 38, 40.5) cm

Materials 6

• 8¾oz/250g, 280yd/260m (10½oz/300g, 330yd/310m; 12¼oz.350g, 390yd/360m; 14oz/400g, 440yd/410m) of any super bulky weight wool blend yarn each in light brown, pink, yellow and blue multi
• One pair size 17 (12.75mm) needles *or size to obtain gauge*

Gauge

7 sts and 12 rows = 4"/10cm using size 17 (12.75mm) needle.
Take time to check gauge.

Back

Cast on 30 (32, 35, 38) sts. Work even in St st until piece measures 8"/20.5cm from beg, end with a WS row.
Inc row (RS) K2, M1, k to last 2 sts, M1, k2—32 (34, 37, 40) sts. Work even until piece measures 14"/35.5cm from beg, end with a WS row.

Armhole shaping

Bind off 2 (2, 2, 3) sts at beg of next 2 rows—28 (30, 33, 34) sts.
Dec row (RS) K1, k2tog, k to last 3 sts, ssk, k1—26 (28, 31, 32) sts. Purl next row. Rep last 2 rows 2 (2, 3, 3) times more—22 (24, 25, 26) sts. Work even until armhole measures 7 (7½, 8, 9)"/17.5 (19, 20.5, 23)cm, end with a RS row.

Neck and shoulder shaping

Next row (WS) P 6 (7, 7, 7) sts, join another ball of yarn and bind off 10 (10, 11, 12) sts for neck, p to end.
Next row (RS) With first ball of yarn, bind off first 2 (3, 3, 3) sts, k to last 3 sts, ssk, k1, with second ball of yarn, k1, k2tog, k to end. Working both sides at once, bind off 2 (3, 3, 3) sts at beg of next row once, then 3 sts at beg of next 2 rows once.

Front

Work as for back.

Sleeves

Cast on 13 (13, 15, 15) sts. Work even in St st for 4 rows.
Inc row (RS) K2, M1, k to last 2 sts, M1, k2—15 (15, 17, 17) sts. Rep inc row every 6th row 4 (5, 5, 6) times more—23 (25, 27, 29) sts. Work even until piece measures 18"/45.5cm from beg, end with a WS row.

Cap shaping

Bind off 2 (2, 2, 3) sts at beg of next 2 rows—19 (21, 23, 23) sts.
Dec row (RS) K2, k2tog, k to last 4 sts, ssk, k2—17 (19, 21, 21) sts. Purl next row. Rep last 2 rows twice more—13 (15, 17, 17) sts. Work even for 2 (2, 4, 6) rows. Rep dec row on next row, then every other row 1 (2, 2, 2) times more, end with a WS row—9 (9, 11, 11) sts. Bind off 2 sts at beg of next 2 rows. Bind off rem 5 (5, 7, 7) sts.

Finishing

Lightly block pieces to measurements. Sew shoulder seams. Set in sleeves. Sew side and sleeve seams. ■

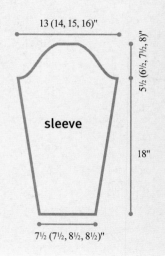

Boatneck Pullover

Made for comfort and speed, this pullover is quick to knit and extra comfy to wear in a soft, bulky-weight yarn.

Sizes

Instructions are written for size Small. Changes for Medium, Large, X-Large, and XX-Large are in parentheses.

Knitted Measurements

Bust 36 (38, 41, 43, 45)"/91.5 (96.5, 104, 109, 114.5)cm
Length 22½ (23½, 24½, 25½, 26½)"/57 (59.5, 62, 65, 67.5)cm
Upper arm 13 (14, 15, 16, 17)"/33 (35.5, 38, 40.5, 43)cm

Materials ⑤

• 4 (4, 5, 6, 6) balls in #362 Quartz of Homespun by Lion Brand, 6oz/170g balls, each approx 185yd/167m (acrylic/polyester)
• One pair size 10½ (6.5mm) needles *or size to obtain gauge*
• Stitch markers

Gauge

12 sts and 16 rows to 4"/10cm over St st using size 10½ (6.5mm) needles.
Take time to check gauge.

Back

Cast on 54 (58, 62, 64, 68) sts. Cont in St st for 2"/5cm, end with a WS row.
Dec row (RS) K1, ssk, k to last 3 sts, k2tog, k1. Rep dec row every 6th row twice more—48 (52, 56, 58, 62) sts. Work even until piece measures 10"/25.5cm from beg, end with a WS row.
Inc row (RS) K1, M1, k to last st, M1, k1. Rep inc row every 6th row twice more—54 (58, 62, 64, 68) sts. Work even until piece measures 15"/38cm from beg, end with a WS row.

Raglan armhole shaping

Bind off 3 sts at beg of next 2 rows—48 (52, 56, 58, 62) sts.
Dec row (RS) K1, ssk, k to last 3 sts, k2tog, k1. Rep dec row every 4th row 7 (8, 9, 10, 11) times more—32 (34, 36, 36, 38) sts. Bind off.

Front

Work as for back.

Sleeves

Cast on 27 (29, 29, 31, 31) sts. Cont in St st for 1½"/4cm, end with a WS row.
Inc row (RS) K1, M1, k to last st, M1, k1. Rep inc row every 12th (10th, 8th, 8th, 6th) row 5 (6, 7, 8, 9) times more—39 (43, 45, 49, 51) sts. Work even until piece measures 18"/45.5cm from beg, end with a WS row.

Cap shaping

Bind off 3 sts at beg of next 2 rows—33 (37, 39, 43, 45) sts.
Dec row 1 (RS) K1, ssk, k to last 3 sts, k2tog, k1. Rep dec row every 4th row 3 (4, 5, 6, 7) times more, end with a RS row—25 (27, 27, 29, 29) sts.
Next row (WS) P11 (12, 12, 13, 13), pm, p3, pm, p11 (12, 12, 13, 13).
Dec row 2 (RS) K1, ssk, k to 2 sts before first marker, ssk, k3, k2tog, k to last 3 sts, k2tog, k1. Purl next row.
Dec row 3 (RS) K to 2 sts before first marker, ssk, k3, k2tog, k to end. Purl next row. Rep last 4 rows twice more dropping markers on last row and end with a WS row—7 (9, 9, 11, 11) sts.

For size Small only

Next row (RS) K1, ssk, k1, k2tog, k1—5 sts. Purl next row. Bind off.

For sizes Medium and Large only

Next row (RS) K1, ssk, SK2P, k2tog, k1—5 sts. Purl next row. Bind off.

For sizes X-Large and XX-Large only

Next row (RS) K1, SK2P, k3, k3tog, k1—7 sts. Purl next row. Bind off.

Finishing

Block pieces to measurements. Sew raglan sleeve caps to raglan armholes. Sew side and sleeve seams. ■

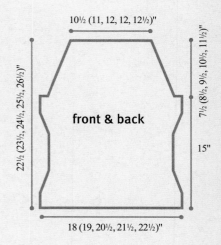

10½ (11, 12, 12, 12½)"
7½ (8½, 9½, 10½, 11½)"
22½ (23½, 24½, 25½, 26½)"
front & back
15"
18 (19, 20½, 21½, 22½)"

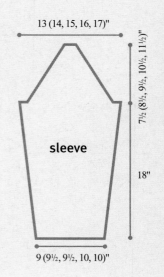

13 (14, 15, 16, 17)"
7½ (8½, 9½, 10½, 11½)"
sleeve
18"
9 (9½, 9½, 10, 10)"

Shawl Collar Cardigan

Garter stitch and gentle shaping make for easy finishing. A three-needle bind-off completes the collar join at the back neck edge.

Sizes

Instructions are written for size Small. Changes for Medium, Large, and X-Large are in parentheses.

Knitted Measurements

Bust (closed) 37 (39, 43, 46)"/94 (99, 109, 117)cm

Length 24½ (25, 25½, 26)"/62 (63.5, 64.5, 66)cm

Upper arm 13½(14½, 15½, 16½)"/34 (37, 39.5, 42)cm

Materials ⑤

• 8 (8, 9, 10) balls in #112 Red of Wool-Ease Chunky by Lion Brand, 5oz/140g balls, each approx 153yd/140m (acrylic/wool)
• One pair size 10½ (6.5mm) needles *or size to obtain gauge*
• One size 10½ (6.5mm) needle for three-needle bind-off
• Stitch holders

Gauge

12 sts and 24 rows to 4"/10cm over garter st using size 10½ (6.5mm) needles. *Take time to check gauge.*

Back

Cast on 55 (59, 65, 69) sts. Cont in garter st (knit every row) and work even until piece measures 15½"/39.5cm from beg, end with a WS row.

Armhole shaping

Bind off 3 (3, 4, 4) sts at beg of next 2 rows. Dec 1 st each side on next row, then every other row 1 (2, 3, 3) times more—45 (47, 49, 53) sts. Work even until armhole measures 8 (8½, 9, 9½)"/20.5 (21.5, 23, 24)cm, end with a WS row.

Shoulder shaping

Bind off 4 (5, 5, 6) sts at beg of next 4 rows, then 5 (4, 5, 5) sts at beg of next 2 rows. Bind off rem 19 sts for back neck.

Left Front

Cast on 30 (32, 35, 37) sts. Cont in garter st and work even until piece measures 15½"/39.5cm from beg, end with a WS row.

Armhole and shawl collar shaping

Note Read through entire shaping directions before beg.

Next row (RS) Bind off 3 (3, 4, 4) sts (armhole edge), k to last 5 sts, M1 (collar inc), k5. Knit next row. Cont to shape armhole as foll: dec 1 st at armhole edge on next row, then every other row 1 (2, 3, 3) times more. AT THE SAME TIME, inc 1 st (M1) 5 sts from collar edge every 4th row 5 times more, then every 6th row twice—33 (34, 35, 37) sts. Work even until armhole measures same as back to shoulder, end with a WS row.

Shoulder shaping

Bind off 4 (5, 5, 6) sts at armhole edge twice, then 5 (4, 5, 5) sts once—20 sts. Work even for 3"/7.5cm for collar, end with a WS row. Place sts on holder.

Right Front

Work as for left front, reversing all shaping.

Sleeves

Cast on 27 (27, 29, 29) sts. Cont in garter st and work even for 6 rows. Inc 1 st each side on next row, then every 14th (12th, 10th, 8th) row 6 (7, 8, 9) times more—41 (43, 47, 49) sts. Work even until piece measures 17½"/44.5cm from beg, end with a WS row.

Cap shaping

Bind off 3 (3, 4, 4) sts at beg of next 2 rows. Dec 1 st each side on next row, then every other row twice more, every 4th row 5 (6, 6, 7) times, every row 4 (4, 5, 5) times. Bind off rem 11 sts.

Finishing

Do not block. Sew shoulder seams.

Three-needle bind-off

To bind off and join collar sts tog, work as foll: Place sts on holders on two separate needles. Hold needles parallel with RS facing and tips of needles pointing right. Insert third needle knitwise into first st on front needle and first st on back needle, then wrap the yarn around the third needle as if to knit. Knit these 2 sts tog and slip them off the needles. *Knit the next 2 sts tog in the same manner. Slip the first st on the third needle over the 2nd st and off the needle. Rep from * across the row until all sts have been bound off. Sew inside collar edge to back neck edge. Set in sleeves. Sew side and sleeve seams. ■

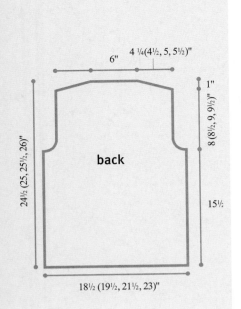

6" 4 ¼(4½, 5, 5½)"

back

24½ (25, 25½, 26)"

1"

8 (8½, 9, 9½)"

15½

18½ (19½, 21½, 23)"

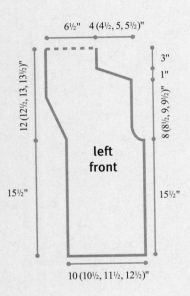

6½" 4 (4½, 5, 5½)"

3"

1"

8 (8½, 9, 9½)"

12 (12½, 13, 13½)"

left front

15½"

15½"

10 (10½, 11½, 12½)"

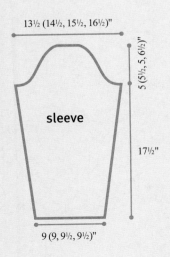

13½ (14½, 15½, 16½)"

5 (5½, 5, 6½)"

sleeve

17½"

9 (9, 9½, 9½)"

Baby Sweater

Who can resist spoiling a new baby? Whether it's your own grandchild or someone else's bundle of joy, cuddle the new arrival with a hand made treasure!

Sizes

Instructions are written for 3–6 months. Changes for sizes 12 months and 18 months are in parentheses.

Knitted Measurements

Chest 19 (20, 21)"/48 (51, 53.5)cm
Length 9½ (10, 10½)"/24 (25.5, 26.5)cm
Upper arm 7¼ (7¾, 8¼)"/18.5 (19.5, 21)cm

Materials 〔4〕

• 1 ball in #00016 Teal(ish) and 1 ball in #0017 Turquoise(ish) of Bernat Sheep(ish) by Vickie Howell, 3oz/85g balls, each approx 167yd/153m (acrylic/wool)
• Size 8 (5mm) circular needle, 16"/40cm long *or size to obtain gauge*
• One set (5) size 8 (5mm) double-pointed needles (dpns)
• 2 buttons
• 5 stitch markers (one different color)
• Scrap yarn
• Sewing needle and matching thread

Gauge

15 sts and 32 rnds to 4"/10cm over garter st using size 8 (5mm) needles.
Take time to check gauge.

K2, P2 Rib

(multiple of 4 sts)
Row 1 (RS) *K2, p2; rep from * to end.
Row 2 K the knit sts and p the purl sts.
Rep row 2 for k2, p2, rib.

Stripe Pattern

2 rnds/rows CC, 2 rnds/rows MC.
Rep these 4 rnds/rows for stripe pattern.

Note

This sweater is worked in garter stitch from the top-down.

Neck

Using MC and dpns, cast on 54 sts. Join, taking care not to twist sts, place different color marker for beg of rnd.

Work in garter st (k 1 rnd, p 1 rnd) until piece measures 1"/2.5cm from beg, end with a knit rnd.

Yoke

Next (set-up) rnd P9 for back, place marker (pm), p9 for left sleeve, pm, p18 for front, pm, p9 for right sleeve, pm, p to end of rnd for back.

Beg stripe pat

Next (inc) rnd Join CC. *K to marker, yo, sl marker, k1, yo; rep from * 3 times more, k to end of rnd—62 sts.
Next rnd Purl.
Cont in garter st in stripe pat; rep inc rnd every other rnd 7 (8, 9) times more—118 (126, 134) sts.

Divide for body and sleeves

Next rnd K 17 (18, 19) back sts, place 25 (27, 29) sleeve sts on scrap yarn, k 34 (36, 38) front sts, place 25 (27, 29) sleeve sts on scrap yarn, knit rem 17 (18, 19) back sts—68 (72, 76) sts for body.
Next rnd P17 (18, 19) cast on 1 underarm st, p 34 (36, 38) sts, cast on 1 underarm st, p to end of rnd—70 (74, 78) sts.
Cont in garter st and stripe pat, working body sts only until piece measures 6 (6½, 7)"/15 (16.5, 18)cm from beg, measured from top of neck, end with a purl rnd. Cut yarn.

Asymmetrical split

Remove marker, slip first 42 (44, 46) sts to RH needle. Join yarn to cont in stripe pat as established only working garter st in rows (k every row).
Next row K70 (74, 78). Turn work.
Next row (WS) Knit.
Cont as established until piece measures 9½ (10, 10½)"/24 (25.5, 26.5)cm from beg, measured from top of shoulder, end with a WS row. Bind off knitwise with next color in stripe pat.

Button flap

With RS facing, MC and dpn, pick up and k 12 sts on left hand side of split. Work in k2, p2 rib for 5 rows. Bind off.

Sleeves

Place 25 (27, 29) sts from scrap yarn on dpns. With MC, pick up and k 2 sts at underarm, pm for beg of rnd—27 (29, 31) sts. Work in garter st (k 1 rnd, p 1 rnd) until sleeve measures 5 (6, 6½)"/12.5 (15, 16.5) cm, end with a purl rnd.
Next rnd Join CC, work in garter st for 1"/2.5cm more. Bind off.

Finishing

Sew button flap to opposite side of split. Sew buttons to flap. ■

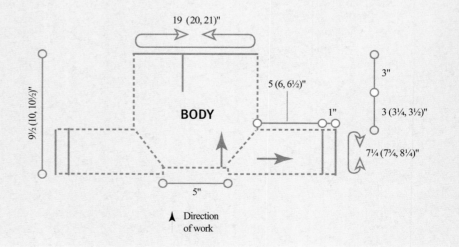

19 (20, 21)"

9½ (10, 10½)"

BODY

5 (6, 6½)"

1"

3"

3 (3¼, 3½)"

7¼ (7¾, 8¼)"

5"

▲ Direction of work

Shawl Collar Pullover

Make this one for your special guy—or yourself! This shawl-collared beauty adds interest for the knitter and the wearer with multiple ribbing patterns and rich colors.

Sizes

Instructions are written for men's size. Changes for sizes Small, Medium, Large, and X-Large are in parentheses.

Knitted Measurements

Chest 40 (44, 48, 52)"/101.5 (111.5, 122, 132)cm
Length 25 (25½, 26½, 27½)"/63.5 (64.5, 67.5, 70)cm
Upper arm 18 (19, 20, 21)"/45.5 (48, 51, 53.5)cm

Materials 🅢

• 4 (5, 5, 6) balls in #152 Charcoal (A) and 3 (3, 3, 4) balls in #135 Spice (B) of Wool-Ease Chunky by Lion Brand, 5oz/140g balls, each approx 153yd/140m (acrylic/wool)
• One pair each sizes 8 and 10½ (5 and 6.5mm) needles *or size to obtain gauge*
• Size 8 (5mm) circular needle, 36"/91.5cm long

Gauge

12 sts and 24 rows to 4"/10cm over pat st using larger needles.
Take time to check gauge.

Pattern Stitch

(multiple of 6 sts)
Row 1 (RS) With B, *p3, k3; rep from * to end.
Row 2 With B, *k3, p3; rep from * to end.
Row 3 With A, rep row 1.
Row 4 With A, rep row 2.
Rep rows 1–4 for pat st.

K3, P3 Rib

(multiple of 6 sts plus 3)
Row 1 (RS) K3, *p3, k3; rep from * to end.
Row 2 P3, *k3, p3; rep from * to end.
Rep rows 1 and 2 for k3, p3 rib.

K1, P1 Rib

(multiple of 2 sts plus 1)
Row 1 (RS) K1, *p1, k1; rep from * to end.
Row 2 P1, *k1, p1; rep from * to end.
Rep rows 1 and 2 for k1, p1 rib.

Back

With smaller needles and A, cast on 57 (63, 69, 75) sts. Work in k3, p3 rib for 2½"/6.5cm, inc 3 sts evenly spaced across last row and end with a WS row—60 (66, 72, 78) sts. Change to larger needles and cont in pat st until piece measures 15½ (15½, 16, 16½)"/39.5 (39.5, 40.5, 42) cm from beg, end with a WS row.

Armhole shaping

Bind off 4 (4, 5, 6) sts at beg of next 2 rows. Dec 1 st each side every other row 4 (5, 5, 6) times—44 (48, 52, 54) sts. Work even until armhole measures 9 (9½, 10, 10½)"/23 (24, 25.5, 26.5), end with a WS row.

Neck and shoulder shaping

Next row (RS) Work across first 13 (15, 16, 17) sts, join another ball of yarn and bind off center 18 (18, 20, 20) sts for back neck, work to end. Working both sides at once, dec 1 st at each neck edge once. Bind off rem 12 (14, 15, 16) sts each side for shoulders.

Front

Work as for back until armhole shaping is completed, end with a WS row—44 (48, 52, 54) sts.

Neck and shoulder shaping

Next row (RS) Work across first 15 (17, 18, 19) sts, join another ball of yarn and bind off center 14 (14, 16, 16) sts for front neck, work to end. Working both sides at once, work even for 2"/5cm. Dec 1 st at each neck edge on next row, then every 12th row twice more. When piece measures same length as back to shoulders, bind off rem 12 (14, 15, 16) sts each side for shoulders.

Sleeves

With smaller needles and A cast on 33 sts. Work in k3, p3 rib for 2½"/6.5cm, inc 3 sts evenly spaced across last row and end on WS—36 sts.
Change to larger needles. Cont in pat st and work even for 1"/2.5cm, end with a WS row. Inc 1 st each side on next row, then every 10th (8th, 8th, 6th) row 8 (10, 11, 14) times more—54 (58, 60, 66) sts. Work even until piece measures 18½ (19, 19½, 20)"/47 (48, 49.5, 51) cm from beg, end with a WS row.

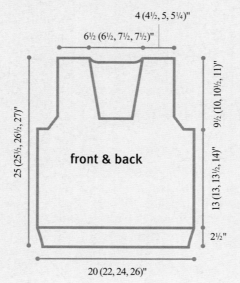

4 (4½, 5, 5¼)"
6½ (6½, 7½, 7½)"
9½ (10, 10½, 11)"
25 (25½, 26½, 27)"
13 (13, 13½, 14)"
2½"
front & back
20 (22, 24, 26)"

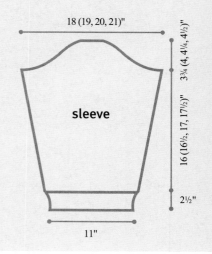

18 (19, 20, 21)"
3¾ (4, 4¼, 4½)"
16 (16½, 17, 17½)"
2½"
sleeve
11"

Cap shaping

Bind off 4 (4, 5, 6) sts at beg of next 2 rows. Dec 1 st each side on next row, then every row 4 (5, 5, 7) times more, every other row 7 times, bind off 5 sts at beg of next 2 rows. Bind off rem 12 (14, 14, 14) sts.

Finishing

Block pieces to measurements. Sew shoulder seams.

Collar

With RS facing, circular needle and A, pick up and k37 (37, 39, 39) sts along right neck edge to shoulder seam, 21 (21, 23, 23) sts along back neck edge to shoulder seam, then 37 (37, 39, 39) sts along left neck edge—95 (95, 101, 101) sts. Beg with Row 2 (WS), work even in k1, p1 rib for 4½ (4½, 5½, 5½)"/11.5 (11.5, 14, 14) cm. Bind off loosely in rib. Set in sleeves. Sew side and sleeve seams. Sew down side edges of collar at center front, overlapping left side over right side. ■

Garter-Ridge Socks

Knitting with five needles may feel awkward at first, but once you've gotten the hang of it, knitting socks can be addictive. This design features a patterned cuff, short-row heel, and self-patterning yarn to keep you interested from top to toe.

Sizes
One size fits women's shoe size 7–8 (39/40).

Knitted Measurements
Leg circumference 7"/17.5cm
Foot length 9"/23cm

Materials ❷
- 3½oz/100g, 330yd/300m of any sport weight wool and nylon blend yarn in blue, green, orange and white stripes
- One set (5) size 2 (2.5mm) dpns *or size to obtain gauge*
- Stitch marker

Gauge
28 sts and 36 rnds to 4"/10cm over St st using size 2 (2.5mm) needles.
Take time to check gauge.

Garter Ridge Pattern
(multiple of 6 sts)
Note Slip all sts as if to purl.
Rnds 1 and 2 Knit.
Rnd 3 *K4, slip 2 wyib; rep from * around.
Rnd 4 *P4, slip 2 wyib; rep from * around.
Rnds 5 and 6 Knit.
Rnd 7 K1, *slip 2 wyib, k4; rep from * to last 3 sts, k3.
Rnd 8 P1, *slip 2 wyib, p4; rep from * to last 3 sts, p3.
Rep rnds 1–8 for garter ridge pat.

Sock
Beg at cuff edge, cast on 48 sts. Place 12 sts on each of 4 needles. Join, taking care not to twist sts on needles and place marker to indicate beg of rnd. Work around in k1, p1 rib for 1½"/4cm. Cont in garter ridge pat and work until leg measures approx 6"/15cm from beg, end with rnd 1 or 5.

Heel flap
Knit 12 (needle #1), dropping marker. Turn work. You will now be working back and forth in St st as follows:

Row 1 (WS) Slip 1, p23 (needles #1 and #4). Place these sts onto one needle for heel flap; leave rem sts on needles #2 and #3 unworked.
Row 2 *Slip 1, k1; rep from * to end.
Row 3 Slip 1, p to end.
Rep Rows 2 and 3 until 23 rows have been completed, end with row 3.

Turn heel.
Row 1 (RS) Slip 1, k13, SKP, k1. Turn.
Row 2 Slip 1, p5, p2tog, p1. Turn.
Row 3 Slip 1, k6, SKP, k1. Turn.
Row 4 Slip 1, p7, p2tog, p1. Turn. Cont in this manner, working one more stitch before the dec on each row until 14 sts rem.

Gussets
Knit across 14 heel sts, then pick up and k 12 sts along side edge of heel flap, M1 between heel flap and needle #2; knit across needles #2 and #3; M1 between needle #3 and heel flap, pick up and k 12 sts along opposite side edge of heel flap; k7. Place marker to indicate beg of rnd and center of heel. Cont to work in the round in St st as foll:

Shape instep
Next rnd Knit around, knitting each M1 st tog with gusset st next to it on each side.
Dec rnd K to last 3 sts on needle #1, end SKP, k1; knit sts on needles #2 and #3 (instep sts); for needle #4, k1, k2tog, k to end of rnd.
Next rnd Rep last 2 rnds until there are 12 sts on each needle—48 sts.

Foot
Work even until foot measures approx 7½"/19cm from back of heel or 1½"/4cm less than desired length .

Shape toe
Dec rnd *K to 3 sts from end of needle, k2tog, k1; k1, SKP, k to end of needle; rep from * once more.

Next rnd Knit. Rep last 2 rnds until 5 sts remain on each needle—20 sts. Combine sts on needles #1 and #4 onto one needle and sts on needles #2 and #3 onto another needle.

Graft toe
Thread a blunt tapestry needle with one of the yarn ends. Hold the two needles parallel with WS sides together. Insert tapestry needle as if to purl into first stitch on front needle, then insert tapestry needle as if to knit into first stitch on back needle. Continue to work as follows:
1 Insert tapestry needle as if to knit through first st on front needle and let st drop from needle.
2 Insert tapestry needle into second st on front needle as if to purl and pull yarn through, leaving st on needle.
3 Insert tapestry needle into first st on back needle as if to purl and let st drop from needle.
4 Insert tapestry needle as if to knit through second st on back needle and pull the yarn through, leaving st on needle. Rep steps 1–4 until all sts are grafted together. If necessary, adjust tension of grafting yarn to make sts even across. Weave in ends. ■

Baby Booties

These far-from-standard booties are knit back and forth on straight needles, starting at the center bottom sole, shaping the instep, and ending with a furry cuff. The resulting piece of knitting is folded and seamed from toe to cuff to create perfect and stylish footwear for baby.

Size
One size fits 6–12 months.

Knitted Measurements
Sole measurements 4"/10cm long

Materials
Version 1 🖐5 🖐4
- 1 ball in #153 Black (MC) of Super-wash Merino Cashmere by Lion Brand, 1½oz/40g balls, each approx 87yd/80m (merino wool/nylon/cashmere)
- 1 ball in #100 White (CC) of Fun Fur by Lion Brand, 1¾oz/50g balls, each approx 60yd/54m (polyester)
- One pair size 5 (3.75mm) needles *or size to obtain gauge*
- 1yd/1m of ¼"/6mm-wide white and black polka dot satin ribbon

Version 2 🖐5 🖐4
- 1 ball in #101 Blossom (MC) of Super-wash Merino Cashmere by Lion Brand, 1½oz/40g balls, each approx 87yd/80m (merino wool/nylon/cashmere)
- 1 ball in #213 Fireworks (CC) of Fun Fur Prints by Lion Brand, 1½oz/40g balls, each approx 57yd/52m (polyester)
- One pair size 5 (3.75mm) needles *or size to obtain gauge*

Gauge
20 sts and 28 rows to 4"/10cm over garter st using size 5 (3.75mm) needles.
Take time to check gauge.

K1, P1 Rib
(multiple of 2 sts plus 1)
Row 1 (RS) K1, *p1, k1; rep from * to end.
Row 2 P1, *k1, p1; rep from * to end.
Rep rows 1and 2 for k1, p1 rib.

Booties
Beg at center bottom of sole. With MC, cast on 28 sts.
Row 1 (RS) K2, M1, k10, [M1, k1] 4 times, k10, M1, k2—34 sts.

Row 2 Knit.
Row 3 K2, M1, k13, [M1, k1] 4 times, k13, M1, k2—40 sts.
Row 4 Knit.
Row 5 K2, M1, k16, [M1, k1] 4 times, k16, M1, k2—46 sts. Cont to work in garter st (k every row) until piece measures 1½"/4cm from beg, end with a WS row.

Instep shaping
Row 1 (RS) K19, k2tog, k8, turn (leave rem 17 sts unworked).
Row 2 Hold yarn to back of work, sl 1 as to purl, k8, k2tog, turn (leave rem 17 sts unworked).
Rows 3–6 Rep row 2, 4 times more. When Row 6 is completed, you should have 15 unworked sts at each end.
Row 7 Move yarn to front of work, sl 1 as to purl, k8, k2tog, turn (leave rem 14 sts unworked).
Row 8 Move yarn to back of work, sl 1 as to purl, k8, k2tog, turn (leave rem 14 sts unworked).
Rows 9–16 Rep Rows 7 and 8, 4 times more having one less unworked st at end of each row. When Row 16 is completed, do not turn, knit across rem 10 unworked sts—30 sts on needle.

Cuff
Eyelet row (RS) K1, *yo, k2tog; rep from *, end yo, k1—31 sts.
Next row Knit. Change to CC and work even in k1, p1 rib for 2"/5cm. Bind off all sts.

Finishing
For each bootie, sew cast-on edge of sole tog, then sew back seam. For Version 1, cut ribbon in half, then weave each length through eyelets around cuff. Tie each into bows, then trim off excess ribbon at an angle. ■